DECODING THE MAGA IDEA

A True Narrative of Freedom and Greatness

DAVID HART

ISBN: 978-1-257-76209-5

Published by: Sharp Press

TABLE OF CONTENTS

INTRODUCTION

The evening of November 8, 2016, was supposed to follow a familiar script. Political pundits had their victory analyses prepared, establishment figures had their concession speeches ready, and Americans across the country settled in to witness what most expected would be a predictable transfer of power from one mainstream candidate to another. Instead, they watched a political earthquake that would fundamentally reshape not just American politics, but the very nature of democratic discourse in the 21st century. As Donald Trump stepped to the podium in the early hours of November 9th to claim an unlikely victory, he wasn't just winning an election—he was announcing the arrival of a movement that would challenge every assumption about how American democracy functions, how political power operates, and how citizens relate to their government.

What emerged from that unexpected victory was far more than a political upset; it was the crystallization of forces that had been building beneath the surface of American society for decades. The Make America Great Again movement, commonly known as MAGA, became the most significant populist political phenomenon in modern American history, fundamentally altering the landscape of conservative politics and forcing a broader reckoning with the health of American democratic institutions. A shift among Republicans moving more into Trump's camp is primarily driving this movement, with a 16-point increase in GOPers identifying with the MAGA movement between the two polls right before the 2024 election (55%) and March (71%), demonstrating how this movement has not only sustained itself but continues to grow in influence and reach.

The Great Unraveling: America Before MAGA

To understand the MAGA movement's profound impact, we must first grasp the context from which it emerged. America in the mid-2010s was a nation experiencing unprecedented levels of political polarization, institutional distrust, and cultural fragmentation. Polarization has increased since the 1970s, with rapid increases in polarization during the 2000s onwards. According to the Pew Research Center, members of both parties who have unfavorable opinions of the opposing party have doubled since 1994, while those who have very unfavorable opinions of the opposing party are at record highs as of 2022.

The traditional gatekeepers of American political discourse—mainstream media, established political parties, and institutional elites—were losing their ability to shape public opinion and maintain social cohesion. Economic inequality had reached levels not seen since the Gilded Age, technological disruption was reshaping entire industries overnight, and demographic changes were altering the fundamental composition of American society. Meanwhile, social media platforms were creating new spaces for political engagement that bypassed traditional channels of information and allowed for the rapid spread of both genuine grassroots sentiment and coordinated disinformation campaigns.

Against this backdrop, significant portions of the American electorate felt increasingly disconnected from their political representatives and skeptical of the institutions that had previously commanded their trust. Rural communities watched manufacturing jobs disappear to overseas markets while urban areas thrived in the new knowledge economy. Traditional religious and cultural values seemed under assault from rapid social change, while globalization appeared to benefit coastal elites at the expense of heartland America. These weren't merely policy disagreements—they represented fundamental conflicts over national identity, cultural values, and the very direction of American society.

The Republican Party itself was experiencing an identity crisis. The conservative movement that had dominated GOP politics since the Reagan era was showing signs of exhaustion, unable to deliver on its promises to shrink government, restore traditional values, or reverse America's perceived decline on the world stage. The party's establishment wing, represented by figures like Jeb Bush and Marco Rubio, offered familiar prescriptions—tax cuts, free trade, and military intervention—that seemed increasingly out of touch with the concerns of ordinary Republican voters who were facing economic insecurity, cultural displacement, and political disenfranchisement.

The MAGA Phenomenon: More Than Politics as Usual

Into this void stepped Donald Trump with a message that defied conventional political wisdom but resonated powerfully with millions of Americans who felt forgotten by the political establishment. The Make America Great Again slogan wasn't just a campaign promise—it was a comprehensive worldview that offered simple explanations for complex problems and bold solutions that traditional politicians had deemed impossible or impractical.

With Trump's victory in the 2024 election, the principles and priorities of the MAGA movement, especially its devotion to Trump, became even more important to Republican candidates and office holders. This demonstrates how the movement has transcended its origins as a campaign phenomenon to become a defining force in American conservatism, reshaping not just electoral politics but the entire conservative ecosystem of think tanks, media outlets, and grassroots organizations.

The MAGA movement succeeded where other populist efforts had failed because it combined several powerful elements: a charismatic leader who could command media attention and inspire intense loyalty, a comprehensive narrative that explained American decline and offered a path to renewal, and a communication strategy that bypassed traditional gatekeepers to speak directly to supporters through social media and rallies. Most importantly, it offered something that establishment politics had failed to provide: a sense of meaning, belonging, and agency for Americans who felt increasingly powerless in a rapidly changing world.

What made MAGA particularly potent was its ability to synthesize various strands of American political thought that had previously existed in tension with each other. It combined economic nationalism with cultural traditionalism, populist anti-elitism with strong executive authority, and isolationist foreign policy instincts with aggressive assertions of American strength. This synthesis created a political coalition that included former Democrats, independent voters, and lifelong Republicans united around a shared sense that America had lost its way and needed dramatic change to restore its greatness.

Beyond Trump

While Donald Trump undoubtedly serves as the movement's central figure and primary catalyst, the MAGA movement is intrinsically tied to Trump, making its future after him uncertain. However, the forces that gave rise to MAGA extend far beyond any single personality. The movement tapped into deep currents in American political culture that had been building for decades: suspicion of cosmopolitan elites, resentment over economic displacement, anxiety about cultural change, and frustration with institutional dysfunction.

MAGA's solidarity with conservative, nationalist and populist movements in Europe has an objective: finding partners for Trump's effort to transform global culture. This international dimension reveals how the MAGA movement represents part of a broader global phenomenon of populist nationalism that has emerged in response to the perceived failures of liberal international order and globalized capitalism.

The movement has also proven remarkably adaptable, evolving from a long-shot presidential campaign to a governing philosophy, from a political insurgency to a cultural brand, and from a vehicle for protest to an instrument of institutional change. Charlie Kirk had a significant political and mobilising influence among the Trumpist youth, demonstrating how the movement has cultivated new generations of activists and leaders who will carry its influence forward regardless of Trump's personal political future.

The Stakes: Democracy in the Balance

Understanding the MAGA movement is not merely an academic exercise or a matter of historical curiosity. American democracy is in crisis. The emergence of affective polarization and populism has contributed to a divided America in which both sides perceive every election as an existential threat to their ways of life, values, and democracy itself. The rise of MAGA represents both a symptom of this crisis and a potential catalyst for further democratic breakdown or renewal.

In mid-2024, MAGA Republicans were substantially more likely than non-MAGA non-Republicans to view political violence as justified and to endorse beliefs associated with violence. This finding illustrates how the movement's impact extends beyond conventional political competition into questions about the fundamental norms and institutions that sustain democratic governance.

At the same time, the movement has demonstrated remarkable staying power and continued growth in influence. Thirty-six percent of registered voters identified themselves as MAGA supporters in the March NBC News poll. It's a significant increase from past NBC News polling — up from 23% of respondents in a merged sample of all of NBC News' polling across 2023 and 27% of respondents in a merged sample of NBC News' 2024 polling. These numbers suggest that MAGA represents a durable realignment in American politics rather than a temporary disruption.

A Roadmap for Understanding

This book seeks to provide a comprehensive examination of the MAGA movement that goes beyond partisan analysis or superficial commentary to understand the deeper forces at work in American politics and society. We will explore the historical antecedents that made the movement possible, the ideological currents that give it coherence, the policy agenda that translates its vision into concrete proposals, and the cultural dynamics that sustain its appeal across diverse constituencies.

Our approach will be analytical rather than advocacy-based, seeking to understand rather than to condemn or celebrate. We will examine both the movement's appeal to its supporters and the concerns it raises among its critics, recognizing that any complete analysis must grapple with the complex realities of contemporary American democracy rather than retreat into comfortable partisan narratives.

The stakes could not be higher. Some divisiveness is natural in a democracy. In the U.S., struggles for social and racial justice have led to backlash and partisan animosity. But the extreme polarization we are now witnessing, especially on the political right, has consequences that threaten to undermine democracy itself. Whether America can maintain its democratic institutions while addressing the legitimate grievances that fueled the MAGA movement's rise will likely determine the nation's political trajectory for decades to come.

The Path Forward

As we embark on this examination, we must acknowledge that the MAGA movement represents one of the most significant challenges to established American political norms in living memory. It has fundamentally altered how campaigns are conducted, how political communication occurs, how policy debates are framed, and how citizens understand their relationship to government. It has also exposed deep vulnerabilities in American democratic institutions while demonstrating the continued vitality of populist impulses in American political culture.

Democrats look at the GOP's 2024 gains and realize they'll be left behind if they don't abruptly change how they communicate. This reactive adaptation by opposition forces demonstrates how the MAGA movement's influence extends far beyond its core supporters to shape the strategies and messages of political actors across the spectrum.

The movement's global reach and influence also demand attention. During the presidential campaign of Argentine President Javier Milei in Argentina in 2023, the slogan MAGA was adapted as "Make Argentina Great Again", illustrating how MAGA has become a global brand for populist nationalism that extends far beyond American borders.

Understanding the MAGA idea requires grappling with fundamental questions about democracy, representation, legitimacy, and change in the 21st century. It demands that we examine not just what the movement advocates, but why its message resonates so powerfully with so many Americans. It requires us to consider both the genuine grievances it addresses and the potential dangers it poses to democratic norms and institutions.

This exploration is essential not just for political scientists, journalists, and policy makers, but for all Americans who seek to understand the forces shaping their democracy. Whether one supports or opposes the MAGA movement, its impact on American politics is undeniable and its influence will likely persist long after current political battles have been decided.

The story of MAGA is ultimately the story of American democracy grappling with the challenges of the modern world. How we tell that story, and what lessons we draw from it, may well determine whether American democracy emerges stronger from this period of testing or succumbs to the polarizing forces that threaten to tear the nation apart. The task before us is to decode the MAGA idea not as partisans or critics, but as citizens committed to understanding the true narrative of freedom and greatness in contemporary America.

In the pages that follow, we will undertake that essential work of understanding, knowing that the future of American democracy may well depend on our ability to comprehend the forces that have brought us to this moment of both crisis and possibility.

CHAPTER 1: THE SEEDS OF A MOVEMENT - PRE-2016 AMERICA

By the mid-2010s, America was a nation in profound transition, caught between the promises of globalization and the harsh realities of economic displacement, between the ideals of diversity and the anxieties of rapid demographic change, between traditional sources of authority and growing skepticism about established institutions. The forces that would eventually coalesce into the MAGA movement weren't born in 2016; they had been building beneath the surface of American society for decades, creating fertile ground for a political earthquake that few saw coming.

The story of Trump's rise cannot be understood without first grasping the transformation that had already swept through American communities, workplaces, and homes long before he descended that golden escalator. This was an America where entire industries had vanished, where familiar neighborhoods had become unrecognizable, where trusted institutions faced unprecedented levels of distrust, and where traditional media gatekeepers were losing their grip on the national conversation. These weren't simply policy disagreements or partisan squabbles—they represented fundamental shifts in how Americans lived, worked, and understood their place in the world.

Economic Displacement and the Forgotten Working Class

The foundation of America's economic anxiety was built on the rubble of its once-mighty manufacturing sector. In June 1979, manufacturing employment reached an all-time peak of 19.6 million jobs, representing the backbone of middle-class prosperity for millions of American families. But by 2016, that number had fallen to fewer than 13 million, with the most devastating losses occurring in the 2000s as globalization accelerated and automation advanced.

The U.S. has lost 5 million manufacturing jobs since 2000, a staggering decline that gutted entire communities and left millions of workers scrambling to find their footing in an economy that increasingly seemed to favor college graduates and knowledge workers. These job losses have likely contributed to the declining labor force participation rate of prime age (between the ages of 21 and 55) U.S. workers, creating a generation of Americans who found themselves economically displaced through no fault of their own.

The causes were complex but interconnected. Between 2001, when China entered the World Trade Organization, and 2018, the growing bilateral trade deficit displaced 3.7 million U.S. jobs, including 2.8 million jobs in manufacturing. The so-called "China Shock" fundamentally altered the competitive landscape for American manufacturers, as companies faced pressure to move production overseas or risk being undercut by imports.

Yet trade was only part of the story. Rising trade with China is often cited as a possible culprit. But competition from China only accounts for about a fourth of the decline in manufacturing during the 2000s. Technological advancement, productivity improvements, and changing consumer preferences all contributed to the transformation of American manufacturing from a labor-intensive to a capital-intensive sector.

For the workers caught in this transition, the human costs were severe. Between 2001 and 2011 alone, the growth of the trade deficit with China displaced 958,800 jobs held by workers of color—representing 35.0% of total jobs displaced by the growing trade deficit with China. These weren't just statistics; they represented families whose breadwinners suddenly found themselves competing in a job market that no longer valued their skills.

The ripple effects extended far beyond individual job losses. We also show that declining local manufacturing employment is related to rising local opioid use and deaths. These results suggest that some of the recent opioid epidemic is driven by demand factors in addition to increased opioid supply. Entire communities that had been built around manufacturing plants found themselves in economic free fall, as the anchor employers that had supported local businesses, schools, and civic institutions disappeared or drastically downsized.

Between 2000 and 2010, nearly six million jobs in US manufacturing were lost, with the sectors most prone to globalisation displacement, such as textiles and furniture, taking the biggest hit. Places like Moraine, Ohio, where General Motors closed its plant in 2008, became symbols of American industrial decline. These weren't temporary setbacks; they represented fundamental changes in how and where goods were produced in the global economy.

The psychological impact was as significant as the economic damage. For generations, manufacturing jobs had provided a pathway to middle-class stability for workers without college degrees. Since the 1960s, manufacturing has always paid substantially more than the minimum wage. Even today, the manufacturing jobs that remain average $20.17 an hour. The loss of these positions meant the disappearance of a reliable route to economic security, leaving millions of Americans feeling abandoned by an economy that seemed to reward education and mobility over loyalty and hard work.

Cultural Shifts and Demographic Changes

While economic transformation was reshaping American workplaces, an equally profound demographic revolution was altering the fundamental composition of American society. Americans are more racially and ethnically diverse than in the past, and the U.S. is projected to be even more diverse in the coming decades. By 2055, the U.S. is expected to have no single racial majority, a demographic milestone that represents one of the most significant population shifts in American history.

The pace of this change was accelerating rapidly in the pre-2016 period. The new estimates show that nearly four of 10 Americans identify with a race or ethnic group other than white, and suggest that the 2010 to 2020 decade will be the first in the nation's history in which the white population declined in numbers. This wasn't simply a matter of immigration; it reflected changing birth rates, intermarriage patterns, and the aging of the white population.

Asia has replaced Latin America (including Mexico) as the biggest source of new immigrants to the U.S. In a reversal of one of the largest mass migrations in modern history, net migration flows from Mexico to the U.S. turned negative between 2009 and 2014. This shift in immigration patterns brought new cultural influences while also changing the dynamics of American ethnic politics.

The implications were visible everywhere, from schools to workplaces to neighborhoods. Most noteworthy is the increased diversity in the younger portion of the population. In 2019, for the first time, more than half of the nation's population under age 16 identified as a racial or ethnic minority. This generational divide meant that America's future was already taking shape in classrooms and playgrounds across the country, even as older Americans were experiencing their communities' transformation in real time.

Religious changes paralleled racial and ethnic shifts. While the U.S. remains home to more Christians than any other country, the percentage of Americans identifying as Christian dropped from 78% in 2007 to 71% in 2014. By contrast, the religiously unaffiliated have surged seven percentage points in that time span to make up 23% of U.S. adults. This trend was particularly pronounced among younger Americans, with 35% of Millennials identifying as religious "nones."

The geographic distribution of these changes created a patchwork of American experiences. Many small communities, especially in the Midwest, have lost white population to out-migration for decades, while new immigrant populations concentrated in specific regions and industries. Immigrants by their sheer numbers have provided a lifeline in many cities that were losing population; played a key role in the growth of places like Las Vegas and Orlando that were becoming major metropolitan areas for the first time.

But the cultural implications extended beyond demographics. Immigrants are invigorating — and indeed remaking — what we think of as our uniquely American culture: the foods we eat, the music we listen to, the films we watch, the books we read. From cuisine to entertainment to literature, American culture was becoming more globally influenced and less dominated by traditional European-American traditions.

For many long-time residents, particularly in smaller communities, these changes felt overwhelming. The uneven growth of the Hispanic population in rural America—the development of rural Hispanic enclaves—provides unusually rich opportunities for better understanding the causes and consequences of rural racial and ethnic change. Places that had been culturally homogeneous for generations suddenly found themselves navigating questions of language, customs, and community identity that they had never before confronted.

The Rise of Anti-Establishment Sentiment

Against this backdrop of economic displacement and cultural transformation, trust in American institutions was eroding at an alarming rate. Just 20% say they trust the government in Washington to do the right thing just about always or most of the time – a sentiment that has changed very little since former President George W. Bush's second term in office. This wasn't simply partisan dissatisfaction; it represented a fundamental breakdown in the relationship between citizens and their governing institutions.

The breadth of institutional distrust was remarkable. Just 6% say the phrase "careful with taxpayer money" describes the federal government extremely or very well; another 21% say this describes the government somewhat well. A comparably small share (only 8%) describes the government as being responsive to the needs of ordinary Americans. These weren't abstract policy disagreements; they reflected a widespread belief that government institutions were fundamentally disconnected from the concerns of ordinary citizens.

Confidence in governing institutions has declined since the 1970s, and confidence in these institutions is now more polarized. Trust in nonpolitical institutions has declined since the 1970s, except for the military. The decline wasn't limited to explicitly political institutions but extended to previously trusted pillars of American society, including science, medicine, and education.

This anti-establishment sentiment was manifesting in partisan ways that would prove crucial for understanding the 2016 election. For the Democrats, confidence is higher than for the Republicans in what we might call the knowledge-producing institutions: the press, TV news, public schools, higher education, and science. For the Republicans, confidence is higher than for the Democrats in the norm-enforcing and order-preserving institutions: religion, police, and the military.

The sources of this distrust were varied but interconnected. Since the 2000s, increasing dissatisfaction with democracy has been a theme of scholarship in both the Americas and Europe. Economic inequality, political gridlock, and a sense that elected officials were more responsive to special interests than to ordinary voters all contributed to growing cynicism about democratic institutions.

American National Election Studies surveys in the 1990s revealed that a majority of Americans believed "public officials don't care what people think" (a sentiment about half of the survey participants shared during the Reagan administration). What was changing wasn't just the level of distrust but its intensity and the degree to which it was becoming organized into coherent anti-establishment worldviews.

The rise of conspiracist thinking paralleled institutional distrust. One of the goals of conspiracism is to activate a general suspicion of hidden elite manipulations. Conspiracist claims are particularly potent as they offer compelling, albeit often simplistic, narratives for how the establishment allegedly maintains control and engages in sinister and secret plots. This wasn't limited to fringe elements; it was becoming a mainstream way of understanding political events and institutional behavior.

Anti-establishment movements or parties are typically characterized by their rejection of some institutions and elites. They often position themselves as outsiders who represent regular people, understand their grievances, and promise to fight against a corrupt system. By 2015, the conditions were ripe for political entrepreneurs who could harness these sentiments and channel them into electoral success.

Media Landscape Transformation and Alternative Information Sources

Perhaps no institutional change was more dramatic than the transformation of America's media landscape. The transformation of the nation's news landscape has already taken a heavy toll on print news sources, particularly print newspapers. Between 2000 and 2015, newspaper circulation plummeted, advertising revenues collapsed, and thousands of journalists lost their jobs as the industry struggled to adapt to digital competition.

Currently, 55% say they watched the news or a news program on television yesterday, little changed from recent years. But there are signs this may also change. Only about a third (34%) of those younger than 30 say they watched TV news yesterday. The generational divide in news consumption was creating fundamentally different information environments for different age groups.

The rise of social media was perhaps the most revolutionary change. Today, 19% of the public says they saw news or news headlines on social networking sites yesterday, up from 9% two years ago. And the percentage regularly getting news or news headlines on these sites has nearly tripled, from 7% to 20%. This represented a fundamental shift from professional gatekeepers to algorithmic curation and peer sharing.

As Stanek adds, "I would probably say...social media changes the way that we connect, or that we don't connect. As long as we're friends on the Internet, we don't have to actually speak to each other, and we just find ourselves scrolling". Social media wasn't just changing how people consumed news; it was altering the nature of political discourse and community engagement.

The transformation was accelerating rapidly. 2010 marked the beginning of the most transformative decade of social media. With UT Social Media Week celebrating its 10th year, let's take a look back at how social media platforms have evolved over the last decade. Platforms like Facebook, Twitter, YouTube, and Instagram were becoming primary sources of information for millions of Americans, particularly younger voters.

In the 2000s and 2010s, the rise of the internet and social media platforms such as Facebook, Twitter, YouTube, and Instagram revolutionized how news was disseminated. Social media has increasingly become a primary news source for millions of Americans, especially younger generations. This shift empowered individual users to become content creators and news distributors, breaking down the traditional barriers between producers and consumers of information.

But the democratization of information came with significant drawbacks. However, this shift also introduced significant challenges for traditional mainstream media. One key issue is the rise of misinformation and "fake news." As social media platforms become more central to the news ecosystem, the ease with which misleading or false information can spread has become a major concern.

The decline of local news has several causes and it predates the rise of the Internet. As far back as the 1950s (and even earlier), newspapers were on the decline due to competitive challenges first from radio and then from television. But the Internet has accelerated the decline. The collapse of local news was particularly significant because it removed an important source of shared community information and accountability journalism.

But social media has diminished the gatekeeping role of media in both audience reach and messaging. LinkedIn, X, Instagram, YouTube, etc. have opened up a massive opportunity in telling your own story and creating your own reach. This transformation meant that politicians, activists, and ordinary citizens could bypass traditional media entirely, speaking directly to audiences without editorial mediation.

By 2015, America's information environment had been fundamentally transformed. The shared national conversations that had characterized earlier eras were fragmenting into countless niche discussions, algorithm-driven echo chambers, and partisan information silos. Traditional authorities—whether journalists, politicians, or experts—found their influence diluted in a digital ecosystem where anyone could command an audience and any narrative could find believers.

The Perfect Storm

By the time Donald Trump announced his presidential campaign in June 2015, all the elements were in place for a political revolution. Millions of working-class Americans felt economically abandoned by globalization and technological change. Rapid demographic shifts were altering the cultural landscape in ways that made many longtime residents feel like strangers in their own communities. Trust in established institutions had eroded to historic lows, creating space for outsider voices and anti-establishment messages. And the media landscape had been transformed in ways that allowed unfiltered messages to reach massive audiences without traditional gatekeeping.

These weren't separate phenomena but interconnected forces that reinforced each other. Economic anxiety fed cultural resentment. Cultural displacement fueled institutional distrust. Institutional distrust created demand for alternative information sources. And alternative information sources provided platforms for messages that traditional media might have filtered or fact-checked.

The MAGA movement didn't create these conditions—it emerged from them. Understanding this pre-existing landscape is essential for comprehending how a political outsider with no government experience could successfully challenge the most established political dynasties in America and ultimately capture the presidency. The seeds of the movement had been planted long before Trump arrived to harvest them; his genius lay in recognizing their potential and knowing exactly how to cultivate them into a political force that would reshape American democracy.

CHAPTER 2: THE MAKING OF A POLITICAL PHENOMENON

The escalator ride down to the lobby of Trump Tower on June 16, 2015, lasted less than a minute, but it marked the beginning of one of the most extraordinary political transformations in American history. As Donald Trump descended that golden escalator with Melania by his side, few observers—including seasoned political analysts, Republican party leaders, and perhaps even Trump himself—could have predicted that this moment would launch not just a presidential campaign, but a complete reimagining of American political communication, celebrity culture, and the very nature of democratic discourse.

What emerged from that campaign announcement wasn't simply another political candidacy; it was the crystallization of decades of media savvy, celebrity cultivation, and political instincts into a phenomenon that would fundamentally alter the American political landscape. The man who stepped off that escalator had spent years preparing for this moment, not in the traditional sense of policy briefings and political apprenticeships, but through a unique apprenticeship in the art of public attention, media manipulation, and brand building that would prove far more valuable than conventional political experience.

Donald Trump's Political Evolution and Early Messaging

Trump's path to political prominence was unlike any other candidate in American history, forged not in legislative chambers or government offices, but in tabloid headlines, reality television boardrooms, and the echo chambers of social media speculation. Trump's overt political activity started with his publicly suggesting a run for president in the late 1980s. Ever since, Trump maintained a steady interest in politics, though he was not always considered a serious candidate.

His earliest political messaging emerged through carefully placed newspaper advertisements and strategic media appearances. In 1987, Trump placed full-page advertisements in major newspapers expressing his views on foreign policy and how to eliminate the federal budget deficit. These ads rehearsed themes that would later define his presidency, particularly his objection to providing military assistance to "countries that can afford to defend themselves" and his broader skepticism of America's global commitments.

The 1988 presidential cycle saw Trump's first serious flirtation with national politics when he approached Lee Atwater, asking to be put into consideration to be Republican nominee George H. W. Bush's running mate. Bush found the request "strange and unbelievable," but it demonstrated Trump's early recognition that his celebrity status could translate into political viability.

The 2000 election cycle marked Trump's first actual presidential campaign, albeit a brief one. Trump was a candidate in the 2000 Reform Party presidential primaries for three months before he withdrew in February 2000. This experience gave him valuable insight into the mechanics of presidential campaigns while reinforcing his belief that traditional political experience was less important than the ability to command media attention and connect directly with voters.

However, it was during the Obama presidency that Trump found the political message that would define his rise to power. In 2011, Trump became the leading proponent of the racist "birther" conspiracy theory that Barack Obama, the first black U.S. president, was not born in the United States. He claimed credit for pressuring the government to publish Obama's birth certificate, which he considered fraudulent.

This birther campaign was politically brilliant in its strategic targeting and execution. Trump gained increasing political notoriety with the public for his promotion of the birtherism conspiracy theory during this period, which has been described as having "essentially launched his current political career." The conspiracy theory served multiple purposes: it challenged the legitimacy of the first Black president, it positioned Trump as a fearless truth-teller willing to ask uncomfortable questions, and it built him a devoted following among those who shared his skepticism about Obama's presidency.

The birther campaign culminated in a moment that may have sealed Trump's political destiny. It was April 30, 2011, and Trump was the recipient of President Obama's jokes at the White House Correspondents' Dinner. Trump political adviser Roger Stone tells that the dinner was a turning point for Trump. "I think that is the night he resolves to run for president," Stone says, "I think that he is kind of motivated by it: 'Maybe I'll just run.'" The public humiliation at the hands of the president and the Washington establishment may have provided the final motivation Trump needed to transform from political gadfly to serious presidential contender.

Throughout this evolution, Trump's messaging consistently emphasized themes that would later become central to his campaign: America was being taken advantage of by allies and enemies alike, political elites were corrupt and incompetent, and only an outsider with business success could restore American greatness. He spoke at the Conservative Political Action Conference (CPAC) multiple times, with his first appearance in 2012, using these forums to test and refine his political messaging.

The 2016 Campaign Strategy and Grassroots Mobilization

When Trump formally announced his candidacy on June 16, 2015, with a campaign rally and a speech at Trump Tower in New York City, he brought to bear fifteen years of political messaging development and media relationship building. In his speech, Trump drew attention to domestic issues, such as illegal immigration, offshoring of American jobs, the U.S. national debt, and Islamic terrorism. The campaign slogan was announced as "Make America Great Again."

Trump's campaign strategy defied conventional wisdom at almost every turn. While traditional campaigns focused on building massive ground organizations, sophisticated data operations, and carefully planned media strategies, Trump pursued what could only be called a reality television approach to presidential politics. Many of Trump's remarks were controversial and helped his campaign garner extensive coverage by the mainstream media, trending topics, and social media.

The Trump campaign made extensive use of social media platforms, notably Twitter, to reach voters. Trump had been politically active on Twitter prior to his presidential campaign, commenting on Barack Obama's presidency and spreading conspiracy theories about Obama's place of birth. He continued to use social media to share his opinions on various topics during his campaign in a personal style, unlike his opponent Hillary Clinton, who maintained a more curated image.

Trump was more active on Twitter than any other presidential candidate of the election cycle, and his unique use of the site led him to be labelled "a social media master," "a virtuoso of the tweet," "genius," and is credited with having changed the role of social media in political campaigning. Unlike other candidates, Trump's Twitter and Facebook posts were often focused on engaging with the public and news media, rather than his campaign website.

The grassroots mobilization strategy centered around Trump's campaign rallies, which became cultural and political phenomena in themselves. Trump's campaign rallies attracted large crowds as well as public controversy. Some of the events were marked by incidents of violence between Trump supporters and protesters, mistreatment of some journalists, and disruption by a large group of protesters. The rallies served multiple strategic purposes: they generated massive free media coverage, they energized the base of supporters who would become volunteer evangelists for the campaign, and they provided Trump with direct feedback from voters that helped him refine his messaging.

Trump labeled competitors with unflattering names like "Crooked Hillary" and "Lyin' Ted" to solicit reactions from the candidates and psychologically repositioned their standing among voters. He also applied a problem/solution marketing formula. He framed the "problem" as the nation being in economic and societal trouble, rallied people to galvanize their dissatisfaction with government and positioned himself as the change agent.

The campaign's use of social media was particularly revolutionary. Trump used social media, and Twitter in particular, to build relationships with voters and create a word-of-mouth buzz for his brand. Clinton's use of social media did not generate as much communication buzz. This strategy helped Trump build attitudinal loyalty, the degree to which a customer prefers or likes a brand, rather than behavioral loyalty, when a customer buys a product out of habit.

Perhaps most importantly, Trump's grassroots strategy tapped into the anti-establishment sentiment that had been building for years. Strategic marketing categorizes consumers into segments or groups of buyers based on behavioral, demographic, geographic and psychographic characteristics. Trump marketed to voters based on their wants, social class, income, ethnicity, location, opinions, values and lifestyles and held events attended by those market segments.

A geographical study found support for Trump in the Republican primaries was correlated positively with the following factors (in order of statistical strength): (1) proportion of white lacking a high school diploma; (2) ethnicity reported as "American" on the census; (3) living in a mobile home; (4) jobs largely in agriculture, construction, manufacturing or trade; (5) having a history of voting for segregationists such as George Wallace in 1968; and (6) residents born in the United States and being an evangelical Christian. This data revealed that Trump wasn't just winning over traditional Republican voters—he was assembling a coalition of Americans who felt forgotten by the political and economic system.

Election Night 2016 and the Political Establishment's Response

November 8, 2016, began as what most political observers expected would be a routine election night. Hillary Clinton entered Election Day with a modest lead in most national polls, and the political establishment was largely prepared for what seemed like an inevitable Clinton victory. Instead, America woke up Wednesday to a new and unexpected reality — Donald J. Trump will be the next president of the United States.

In one of the biggest upsets in American political history, Donald Trump won a truly historic victory in the U.S. presidential election. Trump's remarkably decisive win stunned most political pundits. Throughout the campaign, Trump seemed to have a polling ceiling of about 44 percent and he consistently had the highest unfavorability rating of any major party nominee in history.

The answer lay in the intense and widespread public hostility to the political, media and business establishments that lead the country. Trust in institutions is at an all-time low and a majority of Americans believe the country is headed in the wrong direction. The angry and volatile public mood made 2016 the ultimate change election. Amid such a potent anti-establishment spirit, Trump's vulgar, intemperate and unorthodox style struck voters as far more genuine than the highly cautious and controlled Hillary Clinton.

Trump's night began with critical victories in Florida, North Carolina and Ohio, three states essential to his path to 270 electoral votes. As the night wore on, Clinton's "blue wall" collapsed amid a red tide that swept across the country from the Atlantic coast to the Rocky Mountains. The blue states of Pennsylvania, Michigan, Wisconsin and Iowa fell to Trump like dominoes.

The shock was palpable across the political establishment. "You're awake by the way," MSNBC host Rachel Maddow helpfully pointed out to viewers, "You're not having a terrible, terrible dream. Also, you're not dead, and you haven't gone to hell. This is your life now." The reaction from liberal commentators and celebrities revealed the depth of their miscalculation about Trump's viability and the American electorate's mood.

International observers were equally stunned. Defense Minister Ursula von der Leyen said the result was "a big shock" and "a vote against Washington, against the establishment." The global political establishment, which had dismissed Trump as a curiosity rather than a serious threat to the international order, suddenly had to reckon with a president whose campaign had explicitly challenged many of the assumptions underlying postwar American foreign policy.

According to the authors of Shattered: Inside Hillary Clinton's Doomed Campaign, the White House had concluded by late Tuesday night that Trump would win the election. Obama's political director David Simas called Clinton campaign manager Robby Mook to persuade Clinton to concede the election, with no success. Obama then called Clinton directly, citing the importance of continuity of government, to ask her to publicly acknowledge that Trump had won.

The Associated Press called Pennsylvania for Trump at 1:35 AM EST, putting Trump at 267 electoral votes. By 2:01 AM EST, they had called both Maine and Nebraska's second congressional districts for Trump, putting him at 269 electoral votes, making it impossible for Clinton to reach 270. Trump's victory capped a brutal campaign that left his reputation — and that of his rival — in shreds.

Perhaps most significantly, at a deeper level, the most shocking aspect of this outcome for the ruling elite – including the corporate executives and the political establishment and corporate media outlets who serve them – is that the way they have dominated politics in this country through the two party system is broken. The corporate elite might strongly prefer one or the other but they could live with either. All that changed in 2016.

The political establishment's response revealed their fundamental misunderstanding of the forces that had propelled Trump to victory. Rather than recognizing the legitimate grievances that had motivated Trump voters, many establishment figures retreated into explanations that focused on Russian interference, media bias, or voter ignorance—anything except a serious reckoning with their own failures to address the concerns of working-class Americans.

The Intersection of Celebrity Culture and Politics

Perhaps no aspect of Trump's rise was more revolutionary than his successful merger of celebrity culture with presidential politics. Trump has been in the public eye for over 30 years, which meant that he entered the race with nearly 100 percent name recognition. Trump's longstanding status as a celebrity enabled him to garner relentless media attention from the moment he entered the race.

The foundation of Trump's celebrity was built through his starring role on The Apprentice, which ran seven seasons followed by Celebrity Apprentice, which ran for eight seasons. Trump was already an established reality television star when he launched his political career. At first, pundits just assumed Trump was running for president as a ratings ploy, but to Washington's surprise (and Trump's, if reports are to be believed) Trump has swept 18 states and holds a commanding delegate lead.

The Apprentice was so successful that, according to Trump, he earned $214 million from 14 seasons of the show, plus more from related product licensing as his name as a brand became more valuable. More importantly, the show presented Trump to millions of Americans as "America's Boss"—a decisive, successful business leader who could cut through bureaucracy and make tough decisions.

Research has shown the profound political impact of Trump's reality television career. "I strongly believe that Donald Trump would not be president if it weren't for his being on 'The Apprentice' and 'The Celebrity Apprentice,'" according to University at Buffalo psychology professor Shira Gabriel, who led the first scientific study of how viewers' parasocial bonds with Trump contributed to his electoral success.

Viewers who developed a parasocial relationship with Trump liked him, according to Gabriel. That predicted believing many of his promises, as if trusting the word of a friend. At the same time, the study's results suggested viewers were less likely to believe negative stories about Trump. Since the human brain did not evolve to distinguish between real friends who we seek week after week in real life and characters who we see week after week on TV, these bonds can feel very real.

The Apprentice allowed Trump to build a reputation that would bear fruit for his nascent political career through the ties he established with the viewers/future voters. By providing a deluge of uncontested, seemingly apolitical considerations, entertainment media provides a unique route into the public consciousness. Politicians can't buy the kind of exposure with campaign ads that reality television provides, since viewers know campaign ads are designed as persuasion tools and approach them with inherent skepticism.

Trump's celebrity status fundamentally changed the dynamics of the 2016 election. One study found that by May 2016 Trump had received the equivalent of US$3 billion in free advertising from the media coverage his campaign commanded. This wasn't just quantity—it was quality attention that positioned him as the central character in America's political drama.

The mainstream media frequently referenced The Apprentice during the 2016 election cycle, with the total number of articles that refer to The Apprentice or Donald Trump's former career as the reality TV show host twice as high as the number of articles that mention social security. For every three articles about Trump and immigration, there was one article that mentioned Trump's reality TV program.

Trump's success demonstrated that celebrity culture had fundamentally altered American politics. The traditional pathway to the presidency—through military service, governorships, or Senate careers—was no longer the only route to the White House. Celebrity, properly leveraged, could provide the name recognition, media skills, and public connection necessary for political success.

Moreover, Trump's reality television background gave him crucial skills that traditional politicians lacked. He understood how to create compelling television, how to dominate news cycles, and how to build and maintain audience engagement over long periods. These skills, developed over fourteen seasons of reality television, proved invaluable in the context of modern political campaigns.

The Revolutionary Impact

By the time Trump took the oath of office on January 20, 2017, he had fundamentally transformed American political culture. His campaign demonstrated that celebrity culture and traditional politics were not separate spheres but increasingly interconnected aspects of American public life. Reality television hadn't just influenced politics—it had provided a new model for how political leadership could be performed and understood.

The intersection of celebrity culture and politics that Trump pioneered has had lasting effects on American democracy. It has changed voter expectations about political communication, elevated the importance of entertainment value in political messaging, and demonstrated that traditional qualifications for political office are less important than the ability to command attention and inspire emotional connection.

This transformation was not merely stylistic but substantive. Trump's celebrity-based political approach changed how Americans understand political authority, the role of expertise in government, and the relationship between leaders and followers. The political phenomenon that emerged from Trump Tower in 2015 represented not just a successful campaign but a new form of democratic leadership adapted to the entertainment age.

The making of this political phenomenon reveals how profoundly American culture and politics had changed by 2016. The seeds planted in the previous decades—economic displacement, cultural anxiety, institutional distrust, and media fragmentation—had created conditions ripe for a candidate who could speak directly to voters' emotions rather than their policy preferences. Trump's genius lay in recognizing that presidential politics had become a form of mass entertainment, and he was uniquely equipped to excel in that environment.

As Trump prepared to take office, the political establishment was left to grapple with a new reality: the old rules no longer applied, traditional qualifications were no longer required, and celebrity culture had permanently altered the landscape of American democracy. The phenomenon that began with a ride down a golden escalator had become a new template for political power in the twenty-first century.

CHAPTER 3: AMERICA FIRST - CORE IDEOLOGY AND NATIONALISM

The phrase "America First" carries with it the weight of more than a century of American political thought, representing not merely a slogan but a comprehensive worldview that has shaped the nation's approach to governance, trade, immigration, and constitutional interpretation. When we examine the America First ideology at its core, we discover a philosophy deeply rooted in the belief that a nation's primary obligation is to its own citizens, its own sovereignty, and its own foundational principles. This perspective stands in stark contrast to globalist ideologies that would subordinate national interests to international consensus or supranational organizations.

The beauty of America First lies not in its simplicity but in its profound understanding of what makes nations strong, prosperous, and enduring. It recognizes that true leadership on the world stage comes not from endless foreign entanglements or from sacrificing domestic prosperity for the sake of global approval, but from building a nation so strong, so prosperous, and so principled that it naturally becomes a beacon for others to follow. This is the America that our founders envisioned—a republic that would serve as an example to the world through its success, not through its submission to external pressures or its willingness to diminish its own people's welfare for abstract international goals.

Historical Precedents of American Isolationism and Nationalism

The intellectual foundations of America First stretch back to the very birth of our republic, finding their most eloquent early expression in George Washington's Farewell Address of 1796. Washington's warning about avoiding "entangling alliances" with foreign powers was not born of weakness or fear, but of wisdom and strategic thinking. The first President understood that a young nation needed to focus its energies on building internal strength before it could effectively engage with the complexities of international politics.

The term "America First" itself first gained national prominence during World War I, when President Woodrow Wilson used it in his 1916 presidential campaign to assure Americans that their interests would take precedence over foreign entanglements. This early usage of the phrase reflected the deep-seated American preference for focusing on domestic concerns over foreign adventures—a preference that had served the nation well throughout the nineteenth century as it expanded westward and built the industrial foundation that would later make it a global power.

The 1920s witnessed a powerful reassertion of America First principles following the devastating experience of World War I. The combination of the Great Depression and the memory of tragic losses in World War I contributed to pushing American public opinion and policy toward isolationism. This was not the isolationism of weakness or ignorance, but the considered judgment of a people who had seen the costs of foreign wars and questioned whether the benefits justified the immense human and economic sacrifices required.

The America First Committee, founded in 1940, represented the culmination of this isolationist sentiment, growing to include 800,000 members in 450 chapters. This movement attracted support across traditional political lines, including Democratic senators like Burton Wheeler and David Walsh, alongside Republican senators like Gerald Nye and Henrik Shipstead. The diversity of this coalition—including celebrities like aviator Charles Lindbergh, actress Lillian Gish, and architect Frank Lloyd Wright—demonstrated that America First principles appealed to thoughtful Americans across all walks of life.

Critics often attempt to dismiss this historical movement by focusing on its most controversial figures or by attributing motivations that don't reflect the genuine concerns of the vast majority of its supporters. The core of the America First movement was not ideologically isolationist or antimilitaristic. Lindbergh, in particular, based his opposition to the war on a strategic assessment of how best to weather the great storm. In fact, he wanted a significant American military build-up. This strategic thinking reflected a sophisticated understanding that America could best serve both its own interests and the cause of freedom by remaining strong and independent rather than becoming entangled in foreign conflicts that might weaken its long-term position.

The historical precedent established by these movements provides crucial insight into the America First mindset. As Robert Maynard Hutchins, President of the University of Chicago, wrote in 1940: "If we have strong defenses and understand and believe in what we are defending, we need fear nobody in this world". This sentiment captures the essence of America First nationalism—not the aggressive nationalism that seeks to dominate others, but the confident nationalism that builds strength at home as the foundation for security and prosperity.

Trade Policy as Cultural Identity

Perhaps nowhere is the America First philosophy more clearly expressed than in its approach to international trade. American trade policy under the Trump administration can be summed up in one expression, "America First," which reflected a rejection of multilateralism in favor of measures designed to maintain or stimulate domestic industry. This approach represents far more than mere economic policy; it embodies a fundamental understanding that trade relationships shape cultural relationships, and that a nation's economic independence directly affects its cultural and political independence.

The America First approach to trade recognizes that economic policy is cultural policy. When we allow unfair trade practices to hollow out American manufacturing, we're not just losing jobs—we're losing the cultural foundation that comes from productive work, from the dignity of making things with our hands, and from the communities that grow up around manufacturing centers. The Trump administration recognized that "large and persistent annual U.S. goods trade deficits have led to the hollowing out of our manufacturing base; resulted in a lack of incentive to increase advanced domestic manufacturing capacity; undermined critical supply chains; and rendered our defense-industrial base dependent on foreign adversaries".

The use of tariffs as a tool of America First policy reflects this deeper understanding of trade's cultural dimensions. Trump imposed tariffs on steel, aluminum, and other imports, raising the average applied US tariff rate from 2.5% to an estimated 27%—the highest level in over a century. Critics focus solely on the economic costs of these policies, but they miss the broader cultural and strategic benefits of rebuilding domestic productive capacity.

As political commentator Nick Fuentes observed, "America First is about recognizing that a nation has well-being. There is such a thing as a national interest, as opposed to the GDP, the economy, whatever that means. The nation has an interest. The nation is a whole, and it's greater than the sum of its parts". This perspective captures the essential insight that trade policy must serve the nation as a whole, not merely abstract economic indicators that may benefit some while harming others.

The America First approach to trade also recognizes the importance of reciprocity—the golden rule applied to international commerce. As President Trump stated, he is "the first President in modern history to stand strong for hardworking Americans by asking other countries to follow the golden rule on trade: Treat us like we treat you". This principled approach to trade relationships reflects the broader America First understanding that fairness and reciprocity, rather than one-sided concessions, form the foundation of sustainable international relationships.

The cultural dimensions of America First trade policy extend beyond manufacturing to encompass the preservation of American economic sovereignty. The use of tariffs as leverage, such as the 25% tariffs imposed on imports from Canada and Mexico until they address illegal immigration and fentanyl trafficking, demonstrates how trade policy can serve broader national security and cultural preservation goals. This approach recognizes that economic relationships cannot be separated from security relationships, and that nations willing to allow harmful substances and illegal immigration to flow across our borders cannot expect to maintain privileged economic access to American markets.

Immigration as National Security and Cultural Preservation

The America First approach to immigration represents perhaps the most misunderstood aspect of this ideology, yet it flows directly from the most fundamental obligations of any government: to protect its citizens and preserve the nation's founding principles. This perspective recognizes that immigration policy is not merely an economic or humanitarian issue, but fundamentally a question of national sovereignty and cultural continuity.

The historical precedent for viewing immigration through the lens of national preservation stretches back over a century. The Immigration Act of 1924 limited immigration through a national origins quota system, with the stated purpose being "to preserve the ideal of U.S. homogeneity". While contemporary critics denounce such policies, they reflected a sophisticated understanding that nations, like families, have the right and responsibility to determine their own composition and to ensure that new members can successfully integrate into existing cultural frameworks.

The 1924 Act also authorized the creation of the country's first formal border control service, the U.S. Border Patrol, recognizing that meaningful immigration policy requires meaningful enforcement. This insight remains as relevant today as it was a century ago: immigration laws that are not enforced cease to be laws at all and instead become mere suggestions that encourage further violations.

The America First perspective on immigration recognizes that massive demographic changes inevitably produce cultural changes, and that any nation has the right to manage such changes at a pace that allows for successful integration rather than social disruption. As one immigration expert observed, "Since its founding days, the United States had mostly open borders, welcoming immigrants from across the world to work and build lives here. In the late 1800s, record numbers of migrants from Italy, Greece and Central and Eastern Europe made the journey on newly invented steamships to the United States. Many, especially in America's now crowded cities, began to question the open door policy".

This historical pattern reveals an important truth: immigration policy must be calibrated to a nation's capacity for integration. When immigration levels overwhelm that capacity, the result is not successful assimilation but the creation of parallel societies that may never fully embrace American values and principles. The response to these concerns led to "sweeping legislation restricting immigration" in 1924, with "Congress nearly closes the door, and the part of the door that's open is really just open to Western Europe".

The modern America First approach to immigration seeks to restore this balance between openness and assimilation. The use of economic leverage to address illegal immigration and drug trafficking reflects the understanding that "access to the American market is a privilege" that should be extended only to nations that respect American sovereignty and contribute to American security. This approach recognizes that illegal immigration represents not just a violation of law but a direct assault on the principle of national sovereignty that underlies all legitimate government.

The security dimensions of America First immigration policy extend beyond border control to encompass the complex challenges posed by the asylum system. As experts have noted, "migration from Mexico began to drop, while increasing numbers of Central Americans began to surrender to border control and claim asylum" and "because of immigration court backlogs, this process can take years, and asylees are allowed to live and work in the country until their case is heard". This system creates perverse incentives that encourage abuse and undermine the legitimate asylum process for those with genuine claims.

The cultural preservation aspect of America First immigration policy recognizes that successful nations are built around shared values and common principles, not merely shared geography. The Immigration and Nationality Act of 1952 reflected the understanding that "limited and selective immigration was the best way to ensure the preservation of national security and national interests". This principle remains valid today: immigration policy should prioritize those who can contribute to American prosperity and who embrace American values over those who might undermine either.

Energy Independence and Constitutional Originalism

The final pillar of America First ideology combines the practical pursuit of energy independence with the principled commitment to constitutional originalism. These two elements might seem unrelated, but they share a fundamental commitment to American sovereignty and self-reliance that forms the core of the America First worldview.

Energy independence represents far more than mere economic policy; it embodies the America First understanding that true national sovereignty requires freedom from dependence on hostile or unreliable foreign powers. The concept of energy independence involves "eliminating or substantially reducing import of petroleum to satisfy the nation's need for energy" and is "espoused by those who want to leave the US unaffected by global energy supply disruptions and would restrict reliance upon politically unstable states for its energy security".

The success of America First energy policies demonstrates the practical benefits of this approach. In 2019, "U.S. energy production was higher than U.S. energy consumption for the first time in 62 years" and "the U.S. attained the long-held goal of 'energy independence'". This achievement resulted directly from policies that prioritized domestic energy production over environmental extremism and foreign energy dependence.

The America First approach to energy recognizes that "true energy independence means that the U.S. does not fall victim to the whims of energy cartels, adversaries, or unreliable foreign suppliers for its energy needs. When the U.S. is energy independent, the American people enjoy lower-cost energy and insulation from geopolitical instability". This understanding reflects the broader America First principle that domestic strength and self-reliance provide the foundation for both prosperity and security.

The connection between energy independence and constitutional originalism lies in their shared commitment to the founding principles that made America great. Constitutional originalism, as championed by Justice Antonin Scalia and other conservative jurists, insists that "The Constitution that I interpret and apply is not living but dead, or as I prefer to call it, enduring. It means today not what current society, much less the court, thinks it ought to mean, but what it meant when it was adopted".

This approach to constitutional interpretation recognizes that "originalism is reading the U.S. Constitution the same way most judges would have applied it immediately after its ratification" and reflects the understanding that the founders intended courts to seek "the intent of the makers" by examining the original understanding of the delegates to the state ratifying conventions.

The America First commitment to constitutional originalism reflects the understanding that the Constitution was designed to create and preserve exactly the kind of sovereign, independent nation that America First policies seek to maintain. As originalist scholars explain, this approach is "based on the original understanding at the time of its adoption" and reflects the belief that "changes to the Constitution's meaning should be left to further action by Congress and the states to amend the Constitution" rather than to judicial activism that would fundamentally alter the nation's governing principles.

Justice Scalia's approach to originalism demonstrates its practical application: "While the Constitution must be applied to new phenomena unknown at the time of its framing—for example, the First Amendment's application to radio in the 1920s and today to the Internet—its underlying principles do not mutate over time". This understanding provides the intellectual framework for America First policies across all areas of governance.

The marriage of energy independence and constitutional originalism in America First ideology reflects the understanding that both policies serve the same fundamental goal: preserving American sovereignty and self-determination. As recent policy statements declare, the goal is "to encourage energy exploration and production on Federal lands and waters" and "to establish our position as the leading producer and processor of non-fuel minerals" in order to "protect the United States's economic and national security and military preparedness".

Constitutional originalism provides the legal and philosophical framework for pursuing these policies, while energy independence provides the practical foundation for maintaining the sovereignty that the Constitution was designed to preserve. Together, they represent the America First understanding that a nation can only remain true to its founding principles when it possesses the practical capacity to govern itself according to those principles.

The genius of America First ideology lies in its recognition that these various policy areas—trade, immigration, energy, and constitutional interpretation—are not separate issues but interconnected elements of a comprehensive approach to national governance. A nation that allows unfair trade practices to hollow out its industrial base will find it difficult to maintain energy independence. A nation that fails to control its borders will struggle to maintain the cultural cohesion necessary for constitutional government. A nation that abandons constitutional originalism will lack the principled foundation necessary to resist the pressures that lead to trade dependence, immigration chaos, and energy vulnerability.

The America First approach offers a path forward that honors our history while securing our future. It recognizes that true leadership in the world comes not from subordinating American interests to global consensus, but from building an America so strong, so prosperous, and so principled that it naturally serves as an example for others to follow. This is the vision that has guided America First policies from the founding era to the present day, and it remains the surest path to ensuring that America continues to serve as the beacon of freedom and opportunity that our founders intended it to be.

In embracing America First principles, we embrace not narrow nationalism but enlightened patriotism— the understanding that loving your country means working to make it the best version of itself, and that the best way to serve the cause of human freedom and prosperity is to build a nation so successful in securing these blessings for its own people that others are inspired to follow its example. This is the true meaning of American greatness, and it is the goal toward which all America First policies ultimately aim.

CHAPTER 4: ECONOMIC POPULISM AND TRADE WARS

The story of American economic populism in the 21st century is fundamentally a story about manufacturing—about the communities built around factories, the families sustained by good-paying industrial jobs, and the nation's growing realization that its economic foundation had been systematically eroded by decades of misguided trade policies. This is not merely an academic debate about comparative advantage or economic theory; it is a human story about the real consequences of prioritizing abstract economic models over the concrete needs of American workers and communities.

The rise of economic populism represents a profound awakening to the reality that trade is not just about economics—it's about power, sovereignty, and the basic question of whether a nation will prioritize the welfare of its own citizens or sacrifice their prosperity on the altar of globalist ideology. This awakening reached its crescendo with the election of Donald Trump in 2016, but the conditions that made his message resonate had been building for decades. The economic populist movement that emerged was not born of ignorance or prejudice, but of a clear-eyed recognition that America's trade policies had failed its people, and that dramatic change was necessary to restore the promise of American prosperity.

Manufacturing Job Losses and Deindustrialization

The statistics tell a stark story that no amount of economic theorizing can obscure. From the all-time peak of manufacturing employment at 19.6 million jobs in June 1979 to just 12.8 million in June 2019, America lost 6.7 million manufacturing jobs—a decline of 35 percent. This is not merely a number on a spreadsheet; it represents millions of families whose lives were upended, communities that were hollowed out, and a nation that watched its industrial foundation crumble.

Since 1979, employment fell during each of five recessions, and in each case, employment never fully recovered to prerecession levels. This pattern reveals something profound about the structural changes in the American economy—changes that went far beyond normal business cycles and represented a fundamental shift in how America relates to the global economy.

The scale of this deindustrialization becomes even more apparent when we consider the longer historical trend. Manufacturing employment in the United States of all non-agricultural workers rose steadily in the twentieth century, reaching a peak of 38 percent during World War II. This was the foundation of American middle-class prosperity—an economy where a high school graduate could find a good-paying job in a factory and support a family, buy a home, and build a secure future.

The period between 2000 and 2017 marked a particularly devastating chapter in this story. Manufacturing employment fell by about 5.5 million jobs between 2000 and 2017, with much of these losses occurring even before the start of the Great Recession. This timing is crucial because it demonstrates that the job losses were not simply the result of temporary economic downturns, but of structural changes in the global economy and American trade policy.

The human impact of this deindustrialization extends far beyond the factory gates. A "10 percentage point decline in the local manufacturing share reduced local employment rates by 3.7 percentage points for prime age men and 2.7 percentage points for prime age women". These are not abstract statistics; they represent real people—fathers who could no longer provide for their families, mothers forced to take multiple service-sector jobs to make ends meet, and young people who saw no future in the communities where they grew up.

The research reveals even more troubling connections. Declining local manufacturing employment is related to rising local opioid use and deaths. This finding suggests that the opioid epidemic that has ravaged American communities is not merely a public health crisis, but a symptom of the deeper economic devastation wrought by deindustrialization. When people lose hope for economic opportunity, when the ladder of upward mobility is pulled away, despair follows.

The defenders of globalization often point to automation as the primary cause of manufacturing job losses, arguing that trade policy is irrelevant to these trends. This explanation, while containing elements of truth, misses the broader picture and serves to deflect responsibility from policy choices that accelerated and intensified these losses. Research shows that domestic industries competing directly with Chinese imports saw large job losses, while those in which tasks could be easily automated saw changes in the type of jobs but not their number.

The reality is more complex than simple automation explanations suggest. While research shows that industrial robots have the potential to displace many workers, because there currently are few robots in factories, they can explain only a tiny share of the job losses to date. The focus on automation serves a convenient political purpose for those who wish to avoid confronting the consequences of trade policies they supported, but it does not align with the evidence.

Even more revealing is the fact that for all of 2025, manufacturing employment in the U.S. has sunk by a total of 33,000 jobs, according to Labor Department figures. Most of those job losses have been among companies that make durable goods, such as cars, household appliances and electronics. This demonstrates that deindustrialization is not a historical phenomenon but an ongoing crisis that continues to this day.

Trade Agreements and Their Perceived Failures

The failure of America's trade agreements is not a matter of perception but of measurable reality. These agreements were sold to the American people with grand promises of prosperity, job creation, and economic growth. The results tell a very different story—one of broken promises, shattered communities, and an economic elite that benefited while working Americans paid the price.

The North American Free Trade Agreement (NAFTA) stands as perhaps the most consequential example of this pattern of promise and betrayal. NAFTA fundamentally reshaped North American economic relations, driving unprecedented integration between the developed economies of Canada and the United States and Mexico's developing one. Yet this integration came at a steep price for American workers and communities.

The data show that NAFTA proponents' projections of broad economic benefits from the deal have failed to materialize. Instead, millions have suffered job loss, wage stagnation, and economic instability from NAFTA. This was not an unforeseeable consequence but a predictable result of a trade agreement designed to benefit corporate interests at the expense of working Americans.

The promises made to sell NAFTA to the American people were breathtaking in their optimism and devastating in their inaccuracy. The deal would create hundreds of thousands of good jobs here – 170,000 jobs within the pact's first two years, according the Peterson Institute for International Economics. U.S. farmers would export their way to wealth. NAFTA would bring Mexico to a first-world level of economic prosperity and stability, providing new economic opportunities that would reduce immigration to the United States. Environmental standards would improve.

The reality proved to be precisely the opposite. As opponents predicted, NAFTA has resulted in almost 1 million American jobs lost, this according to the certifications of just one narrow government program. And more jobs are being outsourced under NAFTA every year. Rather than reducing immigration from Mexico, NAFTA disrupted traditional Mexican agriculture and contributed to increased migration northward.

The structural problems with NAFTA extended beyond job losses to fundamental questions about sovereignty and democratic governance. Taxpayers in Mexico and Canada have also paid hundreds of millions of dollars to multinationals through Investor-State Dispute Settlement (ISDS) attacks on environmental, public health, water, forestry and land use rules and toxic bans. These investor-state provisions essentially gave multinational corporations the power to override democratic decisions made by elected governments.

The failure of NAFTA was so evident that it created a broader skepticism about trade agreements that transcended traditional partisan divisions. Recent public opinion polls show broad opposition to the Trans-Pacific Partnership (TPP) among Republicans, Democrats and independents of diverse geographic and socio-economic groups. This opposition was not based on ignorance or protectionist sentiment, but on the lived experience of communities that had been devastated by previous trade deals.

The Trans-Pacific Partnership represented an attempt to expand the NAFTA model on a massive scale. The TPP, a massive agreement with 11 Asian and Latin American countries that is premised on expanding the scope of the NAFTA model. It also contains terms that would more deeply infringe on domestic policymaking matters that directly and tangibly affect Americans' daily lives, from Internet freedom to healthcare costs. The defeat of the TPP marked a significant victory for economic populism and a rejection of the globalist trade model.

The nationalist critique of these trade agreements focuses on a fundamental point: they prioritize the interests of multinational corporations over the welfare of American workers and communities. The division between winners and losers is within countries rather than between them. Under the structure of modern trade agreements, ordinary people in both poor and rich countries can lose, while the wealthy and the powerful win. This insight captures the essence of the economic populist critique—that trade agreements are not about free trade but about corporate protectionism.

The China Challenge and Tariff Policies

The economic challenge posed by China represents perhaps the most significant threat to American prosperity and sovereignty in the modern era. This is not simply a matter of economic competition between nations, but a fundamental conflict between two incompatible economic systems—one based on market capitalism and democratic governance, the other on state-directed capitalism and authoritarian control.

China's rise as an economic power has been built on a foundation of unfair trade practices that systematically disadvantage American workers and businesses. Data shows that trade in counterfeit goods, pirated software, and trade secrets in China costs the US up to $600 billion annually. This figure does not even include the additional costs to companies of protecting intellectual property, disincentives for investment, reduced innovation, and employment effects on skilled American labor.

The scope of Chinese unfair trade practices extends far beyond intellectual property theft. These practices span intellectual property theft, government subsidies to state-owned enterprises, market access restrictions, and manipulation of currency. Each of these practices represents a violation of fair trade principles and demonstrates China's commitment to gaining competitive advantage through means other than genuine economic efficiency.

The economic model of China and its state-owned enterprises (SOE), which are controlled by the Chinese Communist Party creates a fundamental asymmetry in trade relationships. While American companies compete in open markets subject to rigorous regulations and genuine competition, Chinese state-owned enterprises benefit from unlimited government support, subsidies, and protection from market forces.

This economic model creates what economists call "beggar-thy-neighbor" policies. China's regulatory environment poses significant barriers to foreign firms seeking to enter its market. Despite China's membership in the WTO, foreign companies still face restrictions in critical sectors such as finance, telecommunications, and cloud computing. In contrast, Chinese companies enjoy relatively unfettered access to the U.S. market, leading to a significant trade imbalance.

The Trump administration's response to these unfair practices through targeted tariffs represented a fundamental shift in American trade policy. Trump began imposing tariffs and other trade barriers on China with the aim of forcing it to make changes to what the U.S. has said are longstanding unfair trade practices and intellectual property theft. This approach recognized that traditional diplomatic negotiations and WTO dispute resolution mechanisms had failed to address China's systematic violations of fair trade principles.

The scale of the trade conflict reflected the severity of the underlying problems. Between July 2018 and August 2019, the United States announced plans to impose tariffs on more than $550 billion of Chinese products, and China retaliated with tariffs on more than $185 billion of U.S. goods. These were not arbitrary numbers but reflected the massive scale of unfair Chinese trade practices.

Critics of the tariff strategy often focus on the short-term costs while ignoring the long-term benefits of addressing China's unfair practices. A September 2019 study by Moody's Analytics found that the trade war had already cost the U.S. economy nearly 300,000 jobs and an estimated 0.3% of real GDP. While these costs were real, they must be weighed against the much larger costs of allowing China to continue its unfair practices indefinitely.

The Chinese response to American tariffs revealed the strategic nature of their economic policies. China's swift and decisive imposition of a 34 percent tariff on American imports, coupled with tightened export controls on rare earths and the blacklisting of U.S. companies, underscores Beijing's resolve to defend its economic interests against what it perceives as unilateral bullying. This response demonstrated that China views trade not as a mutually beneficial exchange but as a strategic weapon in a broader geopolitical competition.

NAFTA Renegotiation and Economic Nationalism

The renegotiation of NAFTA into the United States-Mexico-Canada Agreement (USMCA) represents perhaps the most significant achievement of economic nationalism in decades. This process demonstrated that trade agreements need not be permanent fixtures that bind American sovereignty to the interests of multinational corporations, but can be reformed to serve the interests of American workers and communities.

President Trump's approach to NAFTA renegotiation was grounded in a fundamental insight that had been ignored by previous administrations: trade agreements should be evaluated based on their results for American workers and communities, not on abstract economic theories or the profits of multinational corporations. President Trump called NAFTA the "worst trade deal ever made" and renegotiated it as the USMCA.

The problems with NAFTA that necessitated renegotiation were not theoretical but practical and measurable. Twenty years after Nafta, both Mexico and the U.S. have seen rising productivity combined with falling real wages. This outcome directly contradicted the promises made by NAFTA's supporters, who claimed that increased trade would lead to prosperity for workers in all participating countries.

The renegotiation process itself represented a rejection of the globalist assumption that trade agreements, once negotiated, must be treated as sacred and unchangeable. During the 2016 presidential campaign, both Trump and Senator Bernie Sanders, an independent, criticized NAFTA for bringing U.S. job losses. After entering office, Trump opened renegotiations to get a "better deal" for the United States. This bipartisan criticism of NAFTA demonstrated that economic nationalism was not a partisan phenomenon but a response to the real failures of globalist trade policy.

The process of renegotiating NAFTA also revealed the extent to which the original agreement had been shaped by corporate interests rather than worker interests. The North American Free Trade Agreement (Nafta) "ignited an explosion in cross-border economic activity," wrote former U.S. Trade Representative Carla A. Hills in the January 2014 issue of Foreign Affairs magazine, reflecting on the 20th anniversary of the agreement. Yet this "explosion in cross-border economic activity" came primarily in the form of corporate supply chains designed to take advantage of lower wages and weaker environmental regulations, not in the form of prosperity for American workers.

The success of economic nationalism in forcing NAFTA renegotiation demonstrated that the supposed inevitability of globalization was a myth. The first signal was when the US unilaterally pulled out of the Trans-Pacific Partnership (TPP) and forced the renegotiation of the North American Free Trade Agreement

(NAFTA). These actions showed that nations retain the sovereignty to choose their own economic policies and are not bound by the preferences of global elites.

The economic nationalist approach to trade policy recognizes that trade relationships must be reciprocal and fair to be sustainable. Protectionist policies conducted by China, which requires the global market to be opened for its companies, but reluctant to open its own market for the global business exemplify the kind of one-sided arrangements that economic nationalism seeks to address. True free trade requires that all parties play by the same rules and provide reciprocal access to their markets.

The broader implications of successful NAFTA renegotiation extend beyond the specific terms of the USMCA to the larger question of economic sovereignty. After decades of increased integration and globalization, global trade relationships appear increasingly strained. Restrictive trade measures are not new, but their rapid proliferation has become the norm as governments actively engage in geopolitical conflicts. This trend reflects a growing recognition that trade policy is too important to be left to technocrats and corporate lobbyists, but must be subject to democratic control and national sovereignty.

The economic populist movement that drove NAFTA renegotiation represents a fundamental challenge to the neoliberal consensus that had dominated American trade policy for decades. This consensus held that free trade was always beneficial, that job losses from trade were temporary and offset by job gains elsewhere, and that attempting to manage trade relationships through policy was both futile and counterproductive.

The success of economic nationalism in achieving concrete policy changes like NAFTA renegotiation has validated a different approach—one that recognizes that trade relationships shape not just economic outcomes but social and political outcomes as well. When trade agreements hollow out manufacturing communities, when they enable massive trade deficits that drain wealth from the domestic economy, when they allow trading partners to engage in unfair practices without consequences, they undermine not just prosperity but the social cohesion and political stability that democratic societies require.

The story of economic populism and trade wars is ultimately a story about the reassertion of democratic sovereignty over economic policy. For too long, trade policy was treated as a technical matter best left to experts and corporate interests. The economic populist awakening represented a recognition that trade policy is fundamentally about values—about whether we prioritize the welfare of American workers and communities or the profits of multinational corporations, whether we insist on reciprocity and fairness in our trading relationships or accept permanent disadvantage in the name of abstract economic theories.

This awakening has not come without cost. The transition away from globalist trade policies has involved short-term economic disruptions, political conflicts, and international tensions. But these costs must be weighed against the much larger costs of continuing to pursue trade policies that enrich global elites while impoverishing American workers and communities. The economic populist movement has demonstrated that these costs are not inevitable, that alternative policies are possible, and that democratic societies retain the power to shape their economic relationships in ways that serve their citizens rather than global corporations.

The future of American trade policy will be determined by whether the lessons of the economic populist awakening are learned and institutionalized, or whether the forces of globalization succeed in reversing the gains that have been made. The stakes of this struggle extend far beyond economics to encompass the fundamental question of whether democratic nations can govern themselves in an era of global economic integration, or whether they will be forced to surrender their sovereignty to the demands of multinational capital and global markets.

CHAPTER 5: IMMIGRATION AND BORDER SECURITY

The question of immigration and border security represents perhaps the most fundamental test of national sovereignty in the modern era. It is the ultimate expression of whether a nation retains the right to determine its own composition, to protect its own citizens, and to preserve the cultural foundations that make democratic governance possible. The America First approach to immigration recognizes this fundamental reality and insists that a nation's first obligation is to its own people—their safety, their prosperity, and their right to live in communities that reflect their values and traditions.

For too long, America's immigration debate has been distorted by false choices and emotional manipulation that obscure the real stakes involved. We are told we must choose between being a "nation of immigrants" and being a nation that enforces its laws. We are told that any attempt to control immigration is motivated by hatred rather than by love of country. We are told that the very concept of borders is somehow illegitimate in a global age. These are not serious arguments but propaganda designed to prevent the American people from asserting their fundamental right of self-determination.

Border Wall Construction and Symbolic Importance

The border wall stands as the most visible symbol of America's commitment to sovereignty and the rule of law. While critics focus on debates over precise mileage or construction costs, they miss the deeper significance of what the wall represents: a nation's declaration that it will not surrender control over its own borders to smugglers, cartels, and those who would enter illegally.

During the Trump administration, the construction of border barriers became a defining symbol of national renewal. The Trump administration celebrated the completion of 400 miles of new border wall system, with Acting Secretary Chad Wolf declaring that "the many miles of border wall system exists because of the will and vision of President Trump". While the total mileage built varied depending on how it was calculated, the impact was undeniable.

Trump's administration built 52 miles of new primary border barriers where there were none before, along with 458 total miles of primary and secondary border barriers. The majority of this construction involved replacing smaller, dilapidated barriers with modern, effective wall systems that fundamentally changed the dynamics of border security.

The symbolic importance of wall construction cannot be overstated. "The border wall system is Exhibit A in showing that the Trump Administration is serious about border security," said CBP Acting Commissioner Mark Morgan. "This wall saves American lives. Every single bit of concrete and steel that goes into the ground stops dangerous people and deadly drugs from coming into this country."

The wall's effectiveness extended beyond its physical presence to its psychological impact on both would-be border crossers and the American people. "We are shutting down illegal border crossing points with the new border wall system," said U.S. Border Patrol Chief Rodney Scott. "For too long, the smugglers had the upper hand in choosing where and when they smuggle their contraband, and that will no longer be the case."

The measurable results of wall construction validated the America First approach to border security. In every region where the wall was built, illegal crossings and drug smuggling plummeted. In the Rio Grande Valley, crossings dropped nearly 80 percent. In Yuma, Arizona, illegal entries were slashed by 90 percent. These were not abstract statistics but real reductions in the flow of drugs, criminals, and illegal immigrants that had plagued American communities for decades.

Critics often focused on the costs of wall construction, but they failed to weigh these costs against the far greater costs of illegal immigration. Building the wall reportedly costs American taxpayers $25 million per mile, but this must be compared to the billions of dollars in social services, law enforcement, and other costs imposed by illegal immigration on American communities.

The wall's importance extended beyond its immediate practical effects to its role in restoring American confidence in the possibility of border control. For decades, Americans had been told that controlling the border was impossible in a globalized world, that walls don't work, and that attempting to enforce immigration law was both futile and immoral. The successful construction and operation of border barriers demonstrated that these claims were false and that a determined nation could indeed control its borders.

The ongoing construction under the second Trump administration demonstrates the enduring importance of this infrastructure. U.S. Customs and Border Protection awarded contracts for border wall construction, with one contract for $309,463,000 to construct approximately 27 miles of new border wall in Santa Cruz County, Arizona, funded with CBP's Fiscal Year 2021 funds to close critical openings in the border wall that were left incomplete due to cancelled contracts during the Biden Administration.

The symbolic power of the wall lies not just in what it accomplishes but in what it represents: a nation's refusal to surrender its sovereignty to global pressures and its commitment to putting its own citizens first. Every mile of wall construction is a declaration that America retains the right to determine who enters its territory and under what conditions.

Family Separation Policies and Humanitarian Concerns

No aspect of America First immigration policy has been more misrepresented or deliberately distorted than the enforcement measures that sometimes resulted in family separations at the border. The emotional rhetoric surrounding this issue has obscured both the legal and practical realities that necessitated these difficult but lawful enforcement actions.

The family separation policy under the Trump administration was an immigration enforcement strategy implemented from 2017 to 2018, aimed at deterring illegal immigration by prosecuting all adults who crossed the border illegally, including those traveling with children. The policy was grounded in the fundamental principle that criminal violations of immigration law should be prosecuted rather than ignored.

The policy was officially adopted across the entire U.S.–Mexico border from April 2018 until June 2018, though the practice of family separation continued for at least eighteen months after the policy's official end, with an estimated 1,100 families separated between June 2018 and the end of 2019. These numbers, while significant, must be understood in the context of the broader crisis of illegal immigration and the failure of previous administrations to enforce the law consistently.

The intellectual foundation for stronger enforcement came from immigration professionals who understood that catch-and-release policies had fundamentally undermined border security. Tom Homan, who was the head of ICE under the Trump administration and had been in border enforcement for decades, was identified as the "intellectual father" of child separation based on investigations into the policy. This was not the product of ideology but of professional experience with the failures of previous enforcement approaches.

The zero-tolerance policy was designed to address a fundamental problem in immigration enforcement: the reality that criminal violations of immigration law had been routinely ignored when committed by adults traveling with children. This created perverse incentives that encouraged the use of children as shields for illegal entry and contributed to the humanitarian crisis of child trafficking and abuse.

A separate family-separation program was run as a "pilot program" in the El Paso Border Patrol Sector from May to October 2017, which resulted in a 64 percent drop in apprehensions while apprehensions began rising elsewhere along the border. This demonstrated the deterrent effect of consistent enforcement and showed that the policy achieved its intended goal of reducing illegal border crossings.

The humanitarian concerns raised by critics, while understandable, often ignored the broader humanitarian crisis created by uncontrolled illegal immigration. The focus on family separations obscured the reality that hundreds of thousands of children were being trafficked across the border, often by adults who were not their parents, in a system that incentivized the exploitation of minors.

The policy mandated that parents who crossed the southern border illegally with children be separated from their children until legal proceedings concluded. This was not a policy designed to inflict cruelty but to ensure that criminal violations of immigration law were prosecuted while protecting children from potentially dangerous situations.

The criticism of the policy often reflected a fundamental misunderstanding of the legal and practical challenges involved in immigration enforcement. When adults commit crimes, they are separated from their children while being prosecuted—this is the normal operation of the criminal justice system. The zero-tolerance policy simply applied this same principle to immigration crimes that had previously been ignored.

Prior to the Trump administration, families were generally paroled into the country to await their immigration cases or detained together. This catch-and-release approach had created a massive incentive for illegal immigration and had overwhelmed the immigration court system with fraudulent asylum claims.

The emotional response to family separations, while understandable, demonstrated the effectiveness of the deterrent approach. The policy sparked a national outcry and changed the immigration debate in America. This reaction showed that consistent enforcement of immigration law could indeed influence behavior and reduce the flow of illegal immigration.

The ultimate resolution of the family separation issue came through executive action rather than legislative change, demonstrating the president's responsiveness to public concern while maintaining the principle that immigration law must be enforced. President Trump signed an executive order that ended the policy of separating immigrant parents and children at the border after six weeks of international outcry.

Merit-Based Immigration and Sanctuary Cities

The America First approach to immigration policy recognizes that immigration policy should serve the national interest rather than the interests of other countries or global humanitarian organizations. This principle is embodied in the push for merit-based immigration and the opposition to sanctuary city policies that undermine immigration enforcement.

The concept of merit-based immigration represents a fundamental shift from the current family-based system to one that prioritizes the skills, education, and potential contributions of prospective immigrants. The RAISE Act seeks to raise wages for American workers by reducing the overall levels of immigration and rebalancing the system toward employment-based visas and immediate family households.

The RAISE Act is similar to the merit-based immigration systems used by Canada and Australia. The RAISE Act reduces overall immigration numbers to limit low-skilled and unskilled labor entering the United States. This approach recognizes that immigration policy should complement rather than compete with American workers and should prioritize those who can contribute most to American prosperity.

The current immigration system is fundamentally flawed in its priorities. For decades, low-skilled and unskilled immigration into the United States has surged, depressing wages and harming America's most vulnerable citizens. Our system does not prioritize the most highly skilled immigrants—just 1 out of every 15 immigrants to the United States comes here because of their skills.

As Attorney General Sessions pointed out, current immigration policies "are not promoting our national interest, but instead select the vast majority of legal immigrants without respect to merit. It doesn't favor education or skills. It just favors anybody who has a relative in America, and not necessarily a close relative".

The merit-based approach would fundamentally change the character of American immigration. The Trump proposal would reshape immigration to the United States by reducing the share of green-card holders who enter as a result of family ties in favor of those selected based on their potential economic contributions. This shift would ensure that immigration serves American interests rather than simply accommodating the preferences of previous immigrants.

Applicants through merit-based immigration systems are usually given a point value according to their age, education, occupation and language ability, a list of characteristics a country values. This objective, skills-based approach would replace the current system's emphasis on family connections with criteria that directly relate to potential contributions to American society.

The sanctuary city phenomenon represents the opposite principle—the idea that local governments can ignore federal immigration law and obstruct enforcement efforts. Sessions argued that "these so-called sanctuary policies force police to release criminals back into the community, no matter what crimes they may have committed". While supporters of sanctuary policies dispute this characterization, the underlying principle remains: local jurisdictions are actively impeding federal immigration enforcement.

The Trump administration's approach to sanctuary cities was based on the principle that federal law must be enforced uniformly and that local governments cannot simply opt out of immigration enforcement. The plan called for cutting federal funding to sanctuary cities—areas where local governments refuse to cooperate with federal immigration enforcement efforts. This move was designed to force local jurisdictions to align with federal immigration policies.

The opposition to sanctuary cities reflects a broader principle of the America First approach: that immigration policy must be made at the national level and enforced consistently across the country. Policies associated with so-called "sanctuary jurisdictions" protect state and local autonomy, prevent federal overreach, uphold due process, and establish important guardrails that keep local resources focused on community priorities, according to critics. However, this argument ignores the fact that immigration is inherently a federal responsibility and that local obstruction of federal law enforcement undermines the rule of law.

The merit-based immigration approach recognizes that immigration policy should serve the interests of American workers and communities rather than the preferences of immigrant advocacy groups or foreign governments. Trump previously supported legislation such as the RAISE Act, which sought to overhaul the immigration system toward merit-based criteria while reducing legal immigration levels overall.

Immigration as Cultural Preservation

The America First approach to immigration ultimately rests on the principle that nations have the right to preserve their cultural identity and social cohesion. This is not about racial or ethnic superiority but about the recognition that successful societies depend on shared values, common language, and cultural continuity across generations.

The cultural dimension of immigration policy is often dismissed as illegitimate or irrelevant, but it represents one of the most important aspects of national sovereignty. A nation's culture—its language, traditions, values, and social institutions—is not merely a matter of personal preference but the foundation of democratic governance and social cooperation.

The current immigration system, with its emphasis on chain migration and diversity visas, pays little attention to whether immigrants can or will successfully integrate into American society. The 1965 Immigration and Nationality Act further solidified the primacy of family-based immigration, which was intended to reassure lawmakers who feared the law's other changes would dilute the distinctly European nature of immigration to the United States. The unintended consequences of this approach have been massive demographic changes that were never contemplated or approved by the American people.

The merit-based approach addresses cultural concerns by prioritizing immigrants who are most likely to integrate successfully into American society. Civics requirements, as proposed in Trump's plan, are also not entirely new. The United States currently requires applicants for citizenship to pass a civics test. Extending such requirements to immigration would ensure that newcomers understand and embrace American values and institutions.

The preservation of American culture does not mean the exclusion of all cultural diversity but rather the insistence that such diversity exists within an overarching American framework. Project 2025 immigration policies propose to eliminate the Diversity Visa Lottery and significantly restrict family-based immigration, often referred to as "chain migration." The goal is to move towards a merit-based system that favors immigrants with specific skills and economic contributions.

The cultural preservation argument recognizes that rapid demographic change can undermine social cohesion and democratic institutions. When immigration occurs at a pace that overwhelms the capacity for integration, the result is often the creation of parallel societies that may never fully embrace American values and institutions.

The America First approach to immigration as cultural preservation is not about maintaining ethnic homogeneity but about preserving the cultural and institutional foundations that make American democracy possible. This includes respect for the rule of law, individual rights, democratic governance, and the shared civic culture that unites Americans across lines of race, ethnicity, and religion.

The wall, enforcement policies, merit-based immigration, and opposition to sanctuary cities all serve this broader goal of cultural preservation. They represent recognition that immigration policy is not just about economics or humanitarianism but about the fundamental question of what kind of society America will be for future generations.

The stakes of this debate extend far beyond immigration policy to encompass the basic question of national identity and democratic governance. The America First approach insists that these decisions must be made by the American people through their elected representatives, not imposed by global institutions, immigrant advocacy groups, or foreign governments.

This is ultimately about the right of the American people to determine their own future and to preserve the cultural and institutional foundations that have made America a beacon of freedom and prosperity for the world. The immigration policies pursued under the America First framework serve this fundamental goal and represent a restoration of democratic sovereignty over one of the most important aspects of national policy.

The success of these policies—from wall construction to enforcement to merit-based reforms—demonstrates that effective immigration control is both possible and popular when political leaders have the courage to put American interests first. The challenge going forward is to build on these successes and to create a comprehensive immigration system that truly serves the interests of the American people and preserves the cultural foundations of American democracy for future generations.

CHAPTER 6: FOREIGN POLICY - STRENGTH THROUGH UNPREDICTABILITY

When Donald Trump entered the Oval Office in January 2017, the international diplomatic establishment braced for disruption. His campaign promises to shake up America's approach to foreign relations weren't just rhetoric—they represented a fundamental reimagining of how the world's most powerful nation would engage with allies and adversaries alike. The traditional playbook of measured diplomacy, carefully crafted statements, and predictable alliance management was about to be thrown out the window in favor of something far more audacious and, to many observers, deeply unsettling.

What emerged over the next four years was a foreign policy doctrine that defied conventional wisdom at every turn. Where previous administrations had sought stability through consistency, Trump embraced chaos as a negotiating tool. Where diplomats had traditionally built relationships through patient cultivation of trust, Trump preferred the shock of direct confrontation followed by surprising overtures of friendship. This approach—what supporters called "peace through strength" and critics termed "dangerous unpredictability"—would reshape America's relationships with everyone from NATO allies to nuclear-armed adversaries. The results were as dramatic as they were controversial, producing both breakthrough diplomatic achievements and moments of genuine international crisis.

NATO: Questioning the Sacred Alliance

Perhaps no aspect of Trump's foreign policy generated more alarm among the foreign policy establishment than his approach to NATO. The North Atlantic Treaty Organization had been the bedrock of Western security architecture for nearly seven decades, yet Trump viewed it through the unforgiving lens of a businessman evaluating a partnership agreement. What he saw didn't impress him: a system where most NATO allies were failing to meet agreed-upon targets for national defense spending, leaving American taxpayers to shoulder what he considered an unfair burden.

The phrase "defense burden sharing" often gets boiled down to "what percent of your nation's gross domestic product do you devote to military spending?" Trump's criticism wasn't entirely without foundation. Most other NATO allies were in the range of 1 to 1.5 percent of GDP, which is officially considered inadequate, and which has been the basis of debate and complaint from the United States for many years, going back well before the Trump administration. What made Trump different wasn't the substance of his complaint—U.S. leaders have pleaded with allies to step up their share of the burden for nearly half a century—but the public, confrontational manner in which he delivered it.

Trump's approach went far beyond traditional diplomatic pressure. He told a campaign rally that allies "are not paying their fair share" and called the 28-nation alliance "obsolete", adding ominously that "Either they pay up, including for past deficiencies, or they have to get out. And if it breaks up NATO, it breaks up NATO." This wasn't diplomatic finesse—it was a direct threat to the alliance's existence if his demands weren't met.

The reaction was swift and alarmed. Trump and his senior officials openly questioned the extent to which NATO could play a useful role in support of the fight against terrorism, a top foreign policy priority for the administration. European leaders, accustomed to American complaints about burden-sharing delivered through proper diplomatic channels, suddenly found themselves facing the prospect that the United States might actually follow through on decades of threats to reduce its commitment to European security.

Yet there's a compelling argument that Trump's confrontational approach achieved what decades of polite diplomatic pressure had not. Trump has already taken credit for progress in defense spending increases, and the data supports his claims. European defense spending did increase during his presidency, though whether this was due to his pressure or broader geopolitical concerns remains debatable.

The deeper question Trump raised about NATO went beyond mere spending figures to the fundamental nature of the alliance itself. US spending on NATO and the defense of Europe amounts to $30 billion, or just over 5 percent of its defense budget, leading some to argue that European "free-riding" was less of a burden than Trump claimed. But Trump's challenge to NATO orthodoxy forced a long-overdue conversation about what the alliance should look like in the 21st century and whether its Cold War structure remained relevant to contemporary threats.

Middle East Breakthroughs: The Abraham Accords and Embassy Moves

While Trump's NATO policies generated controversy, his Middle East initiatives produced some of the most significant diplomatic breakthroughs of his presidency. The crown jewel of these achievements was the Abraham Accords, a series of normalization agreements between Israel and several Arab nations that had seemed impossible just years earlier.

In 2020, Israel and several Arab countries signed the Abraham Accords, with Israel signing similar but separate agreements with the UAE and Bahrain, with President Trump signing both agreements as witness. Trump and Kushner, with the endorsement of the leaders of Israel and UAE, proposed the Abraham Accords, the idea that the three faiths of Abraham—Judaism, Islam, and Christianity—would come together in peace and tolerance in the new Middle East.

The agreements were genuinely historic. The Abraham Accords Declaration emphasized maintaining and strengthening peace in the Middle East based on mutual understanding and coexistence, as well as respect for human dignity and freedom, including religious freedom. The normalization included full diplomatic recognition and intended cooperation in finance, investment, tourism, water, medicine, technology, and other fields.

These weren't merely symbolic gestures. The accords opened up entirely new possibilities for regional cooperation and economic development. The UAE and Israel announced the Abraham Accords, a historic normalization agreement that is transforming the Middle East, with strong bipartisan support in the United States and praise from countries around the world. The agreements expanded beyond the original signatories to include Morocco and Sudan, creating a new axis of cooperation in one of the world's most volatile regions.

Trump's approach to the Middle East also included the controversial decision to move the American embassy from Tel Aviv to Jerusalem. He moved the U.S. embassy from Tel Aviv to Jerusalem in 2017 and then recognized Jerusalem as Israel's capital. Critics warned this would trigger widespread violence, but The Trump administration claimed the alarmists were wrong—that the move would not trigger serious violence.

The embassy move represented classic Trump foreign policy: a dramatic break with decades of careful diplomatic positioning in favor of a bold unilateral action. Previous administrations had avoided such provocative steps, but Trump calculated that the benefits—particularly in terms of demonstrating unwavering support for a key ally—outweighed the risks.

However, critics argued that these achievements came at a cost. The accords bypassed several conflicts, including the Israeli-Palestinian conflict, and did not achieve peace across the Middle East. The Trump administration went out of its way to humiliate the Palestinians, undermining the Palestinian national project at every turn, cutting funding and closing diplomatic channels that might have been used to address broader regional grievances.

North Korea: The Art of Personal Diplomacy

Perhaps no aspect of Trump's foreign policy was more dramatic—or more personally driven—than his approach to North Korea. The relationship began with mutual insults and threats of nuclear war, with President Trump calling Kim Jong Un the "Little Rocket Man" while North Korea referred to Trump as a "dotard". Yet within months, this war of words transformed into an unprecedented diplomatic opening.

The summit with Donald Trump in Singapore in June 2018 made history, as Kim Jong Un became the first North Korean leader to meet a sitting U.S. president—a feat neither his father nor his grandfather achieved. This wasn't just diplomatic theater; it represented a genuine attempt to resolve one of the world's most intractable security challenges through direct leader-to-leader engagement.

The Singapore summit established a framework for engagement. The DPRK committed to work toward complete denuclearization of the Korean Peninsula, while the United States and the DPRK committed to recovering POW/MIA remains. Trump said the agreements would "serve as the foundation for a comprehensive peace across the entire region".

Trump's approach was intensely personal. Trump mentioned that the two had "fallen in love" after receiving a "beautiful" letter from Kim, and he even showed a short film on North Korea's potential for property development during their first summit meeting. This wasn't traditional diplomacy—it was Trump applying his dealmaker mentality to nuclear negotiations, complete with visual presentations about economic opportunities.

The diplomatic process continued with a second summit in Hanoi in 2019, though this ended without agreement. Kim Jong Un assessed that the closure of the Yongbyon nuclear facility would be the beginning of full denuclearization, but Trump rejected Kim's proposal to dismantle the facility in return for lifting sanctions, choosing instead to walk away. A third meeting at the Korean DMZ was more ceremonial, with Trump becoming the first sitting U.S. president to step foot inside North Korea.

The results of Trump's North Korea diplomacy remain contested. The summits themselves delivered little of substance for either side. Kim offered the same vague commitment to denuclearization his predecessors had given, and by the end of Trump's term, the talks had petered out and he had little more to show for his efforts than a drawer full of flattering letters.

Yet supporters argue that the engagement prevented a potential military conflict. The three US-North Korea leadership summits were historic and prevented possible military action in Korea, even if they didn't achieve the ultimate goal of denuclearization. The approach demonstrated Trump's willingness to engage directly with adversaries in ways that previous presidents had been unwilling to attempt.

Russia and Iran: Maximum Pressure Meets Strategic Ambiguity

Trump's approach to America's primary adversaries—Russia and Iran—revealed both the strengths and contradictions of his foreign policy approach. On paper, his administration took a tough stance against both nations, but Trump's personal relationships and statements often seemed to undermine his own policies.

With Iran, Trump pursued what his administration called "maximum pressure." In May 2018, Trump withdrew the United States from the Joint Comprehensive Plan of Action (JCPOA), known as the Iran nuclear deal, and proceeded to launch a "maximum pressure" campaign defined by the sweeping use of unilateral sanctions against Iran. Trump argued that "It is clear to me that we cannot prevent an Iranian nuclear bomb under the decaying and rotten structure of the current agreement".

The strategy was designed to force Iran back to the negotiating table for what Trump promised would be a "better deal." President Trump made clear that Iran must never develop a nuclear weapon, cease developing nuclear-capable missiles, stop proliferating ballistic missiles to others, cease support for terrorists and extremists, end its quest to destroy Israel, and stop threats to freedom of navigation.

The results were mixed at best. The Trump administration's approach erred in two crucial assumptions. The first was that Iran would not respond to U.S. sanctions by expanding its nuclear activity. Instead, Iran announced on May 8 that it would no longer adhere to JCPOA limits on stockpiling heavy water and low-enriched uranium, and by the end of Trump's presidency, Iran's proximity to a nuclear weapon capability had gradually increased, and Iran was roughly six months away from having enough weapons-grade fissile material for a nuclear bomb. When President Trump took office, Iran was about a year from that milestone.

On Russia, Trump's record was even more complex. The Trump administration's policy actions often seemed at odds with the President's rhetoric. While Trump frequently praised Vladimir Putin personally and questioned the value of sanctions, his administration actually imposed significant penalties on Russia. 52 people and entities from Russia, Ukraine, Uzbekistan, and elsewhere were sanctioned for alleged human rights violations and corruption, and the U.S. administration approved a plan to provide Ukraine with enhanced defensive capabilities to help it fight off Russia-backed separatists.

This created a persistent tension in Trump's approach to Russia. President Trump signed into law the Countering America's Adversaries Through Sanctions act (CAATSA), enacting new sanctions on Russia, Iran, and North Korea, even as he maintained that he could develop a productive relationship with Putin personally.

During his second presidency, this tension has become even more pronounced. Trump would never have begun the process if he did not believe that he had a special relationship with Putin that would enable him to persuade him to end the war in Ukraine. Yet Trump has repeatedly threatened to punish Russia with new sanctions if it refuses to reach an agreement with Ukraine, but has failed to follow through as Moscow has ignored several deadlines.

The Unpredictability Doctrine

What unified all of these diverse foreign policy approaches was Trump's fundamental belief in the power of unpredictability. Where traditional diplomacy emphasized consistency and predictability as sources of stability, Trump saw them as sources of weakness. His theory was that adversaries and allies alike had grown too comfortable with American responses, allowing them to game the system to their advantage.

This approach yielded both significant successes and notable failures. The Abraham Accords represented a genuine breakthrough that had eluded previous administrations, achieved through Trump's willingness to abandon traditional diplomatic formulas. His direct engagement with Kim Jong Un, while ultimately unsuccessful, demonstrated a creative approach to diplomacy that broke decades of deadlock.

Yet the same unpredictability that enabled these breakthroughs also created new problems. NATO allies found themselves uncertain about American commitments, while adversaries like Iran responded to maximum pressure not with capitulation but with escalation. Trump's personal relationships with authoritarian leaders often seemed to conflict with his administration's policies, creating confusion about America's true intentions.

The ultimate judgment on Trump's foreign policy doctrine may depend on one's perspective on the proper role of American power in the world. Supporters argue that his willingness to challenge established orthodoxies and apply business-like pressure to international relationships produced results that decades of traditional diplomacy had failed to achieve. Critics contend that his approach undermined the careful relationships and institutions that had provided global stability for generations.

What seems clear is that Trump's approach to foreign policy was genuinely revolutionary, representing a fundamental break with the assumptions that had guided American diplomacy since World War II. Whether that revolution ultimately strengthened or weakened American interests remains a subject of intense debate, but its impact on the international order was undeniably profound.

The MAGA approach to foreign policy reflected a core belief that America had been taken advantage of by both allies and adversaries who had grown comfortable with predictable American responses. Through a combination of economic pressure, personal diplomacy, and strategic unpredictability, Trump sought to reestablish what he saw as proper respect for American power and interests. The results were as dramatic as they were controversial, reshaping relationships from the NATO alliance to the Middle East in ways that continue to influence global politics today.

CHAPTER 7: LAW, ORDER, AND CONSTITUTIONAL VALUES

In the pantheon of American political movements, few have wielded constitutional principles as both shield and sword with the effectiveness of the MAGA coalition. While critics often portrayed Trump's approach to governance as norm-breaking or constitutionally questionable, his supporters saw something entirely different: a president finally willing to defend the foundational values that had made America great, even when doing so required challenging the very institutions that had, in their view, strayed from their original purpose. This wasn't mere political theater—it represented a fundamental philosophical clash over what the Constitution means and who gets to define American values in the 21st century.

The Trump approach to law, order, and constitutional interpretation rested on four interconnected pillars: unwavering support for law enforcement through the "Back the Blue" movement, an absolutist defense of Second Amendment rights, a transformative judicial philosophy aimed at reshaping American jurisprudence for generations, and an aggressive protection of religious liberty that sought to restore what supporters saw as Christianity's rightful place in American public life. Each of these elements reinforced the others, creating a comprehensive worldview that challenged decades of liberal legal and cultural orthodoxy. What emerged wasn't just policy change—it was a constitutional counterrevolution that promised to fundamentally alter how Americans understood their rights, their government, and their national identity.

Police Reform Debates and "Back the Blue" Sentiment

The summer of 2020 marked one of the most significant inflection points in modern American law enforcement, as massive protests following George Floyd's death sparked a national reckoning over police practices. While many political leaders scrambled to find middle ground between reform advocates and law enforcement supporters, Donald Trump's position was characteristically unambiguous: America needed more support for police, not less. This stance, crystallized in the "Back the Blue" movement, would become central to the MAGA vision of law and order.

Trump's approach to policing represented a sharp departure from the reform-minded policies that had gained momentum during the Obama years. Hours into his return to the Oval Office, President Trump revoked an executive order that aimed to "advance effective, accountable policing and criminal justice practices to enhance public trust and public safety." But Trump did not just reverse his predecessor's reforms—he also reversed policies that he had championed during his first term, highlighting the political pressure he faced during the summer of 2020.

During his first presidency, Trump had actually signed significant police reform measures. The Executive Order on Safe Policing for Safe Communities mandated that police departments will receive accredited training on de-escalation, use of force and community engagement. Additionally, a database will track police officers within the U.S. who have received complaints of excessive force. This represented a recognition that reform and public safety weren't mutually exclusive—a position Trump articulated clearly at the time: "Reducing crime and raising [police] standards are not opposite goals. They're not mutually exclusive."

However, in his second term, Trump took a markedly different approach. The Trump administration is putting a halt to agreements that require reforms of police departments where the Justice Department found a pattern of misconduct, according to a memo issued Wednesday. The memo ordered the Justice Department's civil rights division to "not execute or finalize any settlements or consent decrees approved prior to January 20, 2025." This move had the potential to upend police reform efforts in Minneapolis and Louisville, Kentucky, which were announced by the Justice Department in the closing weeks of the Biden administration.

The philosophical foundation of Trump's "Back the Blue" approach rested on several key premises. First, that American police officers were fundamentally honorable public servants being unfairly demonized by liberal politicians and media. "An attack on law enforcement is an attack on all Americans," Donald Trump said in his speech accepting the Republican presidential nomination. "I have a message to every last person threatening the peace on our streets and the safety of our police: When I take the oath of office next year, I will restore law and order to our country."

Second, Trump argued that crime and disorder were fundamentally problems of insufficient enforcement rather than systemic issues requiring structural reform. "Safe communities rely on the backbone and heroism of a tough and well-equipped police force," Trump declared in an executive order. "When local leaders demonize law enforcement and impose legal and political handcuffs that make aggressively enforcing the law impossible, crime thrives and innocent citizens and small business owners suffer."

This approach manifested in concrete policy changes. Trump killed the National Law Enforcement Accountability Database on his first day back in office. A compilation of the disciplinary records of nearly 150,000 federal law enforcement officers dating back to 2018, the database had afforded all 90 executive branch agencies the ability to check officers' disciplinary histories when making hiring decisions—a tool specifically designed to prevent the "wandering officer" problem of misconduct-prone officers moving between departments.

Trump also rescinded requirements for federal law enforcement officers to wear body cameras, a policy that had been seen as a basic transparency measure. These reversals sent a clear signal about the administration's priorities: law enforcement agencies would receive maximum support and minimum oversight from the federal government.

The practical implications of this approach were significant. Federal investigators had identified at least eight police departments with patterns of unlawful behavior. But Trump's freeze on oversight activities leaves many reform efforts in the hands of local leaders. In cities like Minneapolis, Louisville, and Phoenix, where federal investigations had found serious problems including excessive force, racial discrimination, and inadequate supervision, the withdrawal of federal oversight meant reform would depend entirely on local political will.

Yet Trump's supporters argued this approach reflected important constitutional principles about federalism and local control. They contended that policing was fundamentally a local responsibility, and that federal interference—however well-intentioned—represented an overreach that undermined both effective law enforcement and constitutional governance. "Back the Blue" wasn't just about supporting police officers; it was about defending a vision of law and order where clear rules were strictly enforced by respected authorities.

Second Amendment Rights and Gun Culture

If police were the thin blue line protecting American communities, then an armed citizenry represented the ultimate bulwark of American freedom in Trump's constitutional philosophy. The Second Amendment wasn't just another right to be balanced against competing interests—it was the right that guaranteed all others, and Trump's approach to gun policy reflected this absolutist perspective.

"Promises made to law-abiding gun owners are being kept by President Donald J. Trump," said Doug Hamlin, NRA Executive Vice President and CEO. "NRA members were instrumental, turning out in record numbers to secure his victory, and he is proving worthy of their votes, faith, and confidence in his first days in office." This statement, made after Trump signed an executive order protecting Second Amendment rights, captured the symbiotic relationship between the MAGA movement and gun rights advocates.

Trump's approach to the Second Amendment represented a comprehensive effort to roll back what he saw as decades of incremental infringement on Americans' constitutional rights. The order directs the Attorney General to conduct a report and make recommendations to better protect the Second Amendment. Specifically, the order requires the Attorney General to evaluate actions taken by the Biden Administration that restricted firearms rights and recommend solutions to undo those actions.

But Trump's gun rights agenda went beyond merely undoing his predecessor's policies. President Trump has gone further than simply moving towards eliminating the anti-gun actions of the last administration. The order further requires the Attorney General to take an all-of-government review to further enhance firearm rights by addressing the litigation position of the United States in any case impacting the Second Amendment, reviewing government classifications of firearms and ammunition, and evaluating wait times for various federal approvals that are required to make, manufacture, transfer, or export firearms and ammunition.

This comprehensive approach reflected Trump's belief that the federal government should be actively promoting gun rights rather than merely tolerating them. Trump has wasted no time on this front. The Trump administration effectively shuttered the White House Office of Gun Violence Prevention, a partisan office created by Biden that employed gun-control advocates. In contrast, Trump has created a Second Amendment Task Force, led by Attorney General Pam Bondi.

The gun rights community responded enthusiastically to these efforts. GOA announced it is "ready to help President Trump execute his promises to restore gun rights," and highlighted pledges to repeal Biden-era ATF rules, fire the ATF director, and pass national carry reciprocity. The Gun Owners of America, generally considered more hardline than the NRA, found Trump's approach aligned with their vision of maximum Second Amendment protection.

One of the most significant aspects of Trump's gun rights agenda was the restoration of rights for previously prohibited persons. On March 20, the U.S. Department of Justice (DOJ) published an interim final rule entitled, Withdrawing the Attorney General's Delegation of Authority. That bland title belies the historic nature of the measure, which is aimed at reviving a provision of federal law that could, for the first time since 1992, allow federally prohibited persons to petition for restoration of their Second Amendment rights.

This represented a fundamental shift in how the government approached gun rights. Rather than viewing gun ownership as a privilege to be carefully regulated, Trump's approach treated it as a fundamental right that could only be restricted under the most extreme circumstances, and even then with opportunities for restoration. NRA has long advocated for the proposition that if a person is safe enough to be free of government restraint on his or her freedom, that person is presumptively safe enough to exercise fundamental rights, including the right to keep and bear arms.

Trump's rhetoric on guns was characteristically uncompromising. "I stand before you with a simple promise; your Second Amendment will always be safe with me as your president. When I'm back in the Oval Office, no one will lay a finger on your firearms," said Trump at the 2024 NRA Great American

Outdoor Show in Harrisburg, Pa. This wasn't just campaign rhetoric—it reflected a genuine philosophical commitment to gun rights as the foundation of American freedom.

However, this absolutist approach was tested when the administration reportedly considered restrictions on transgender individuals' gun rights. "The NRA supports the Second Amendment rights of all law abiding Americans to purchase, possess and use firearms," the organization said in a social media post. "NRA does not, and will not, support any policy proposals that implement sweeping gun bans that arbitrarily strip law-abiding citizens of their Second Amendment rights without due process." The fact that gun rights groups pushed back against Trump showed the consistency of their principles—Second Amendment rights were universal rights, not privileges to be granted or withheld based on political considerations.

The broader gun culture that emerged around Trump's movement reflected deep-seated beliefs about American identity. Gun ownership wasn't just about self-defense or hunting—it represented independence, self-reliance, and skepticism of government power. In the MAGA worldview, an armed citizenry served as the ultimate check on tyranny, a principle they argued was validated by recent history from Hong Kong to Ukraine.

Judicial Philosophy and Supreme Court Appointments

While Trump's policy victories could be reversed by future administrations, his transformation of the American judiciary represented a generational achievement that would shape constitutional interpretation for decades to come. The three Supreme Court justices he appointed—Neil Gorsuch, Brett Kavanaugh, and Amy Coney Barrett—along with more than 230 lower court judges, represented the most comprehensive judicial realignment since Franklin Roosevelt's presidency.

Trump also had a major influence on the nation's highest court. The three Supreme Court justices he appointed – Neil Gorsuch, Brett Kavanaugh and Amy Coney Barrett – are the most by any president since Ronald Reagan (who appointed four) and the most by any one-term president since Herbert Hoover. These appointments fundamentally altered the court's ideological balance, creating a 6-3 conservative majority that would endure well beyond Trump's presidency.

The strategic approach to judicial appointments reflected careful planning by conservative legal organizations. During the 2016 presidential election campaign, candidate Donald Trump took the unprecedented move of releasing a list of his potential Supreme Court nominees. But Trump didn't assemble this list himself. Instead, he outsourced the selection of his judicial appointments to leaders of the Federalist Society, an organization in the conservative legal movement. As Trump explained: "We're going to have great judges, conservative, all picked by the Federalist Society."

This partnership with the Federalist Society proved transformational. In his first presidential term, Trump appointed three justices affiliated with the Federalist Society – Neil Gorsuch, Brett Kavanaugh, and Amy Coney Barrett – in addition to hundreds of lower federal court judges. The Federalist Society's influence extended far beyond the Supreme Court, as Trump appointed Federalist Society members to appeals courts and district courts across the country.

The judicial philosophy underlying these appointments emphasized originalism and textualism—the ideas that constitutional and statutory interpretation should focus on the original meaning of the text rather than evolving contemporary values. This represented a direct challenge to the "living Constitution" approach that had dominated liberal jurisprudence for decades. Conservative legal scholars argued that this approach would constrain judicial activism and restore democratic accountability to American governance.

The results were immediately apparent. Trump's judicial appointments played crucial roles in overturning Roe v. Wade, expanding religious liberty protections, constraining federal regulatory power, and strengthening Second Amendment rights. These weren't just policy victories for conservatives—they represented a fundamental shift in constitutional interpretation that would influence American law for generations.

However, Trump's relationship with his judicial appointees was more complex than simple loyalty. These losses illustrate how, even as major new legal issues involving Trump reach the justices, he does not always receive a warm reception at the court he helped shape with his appointments of Justices Neil Gorsuch, Brett Kavanaugh and Amy Coney Barrett, ensuring a 6-3 conservative majority. When Trump faced legal challenges as a former president, his appointees didn't provide blanket protection—they ruled based on their understanding of the law rather than personal loyalty.

This independence actually validated the conservative legal movement's approach to judicial appointments. The justices themselves "understand well, even if Mr. Trump does not, that their role is to interpret the law, not to protect any particular public figure's personal interests," said Richard Garnett, a professor at Notre Dame Law School. The fact that Trump's appointees ruled against him in some cases demonstrated their commitment to judicial principles over political considerations.

In his second term, Trump signaled a shift in his judicial selection criteria. President Donald Trump is signaling a new approach to selecting judges in his second term, departing from his first-term formula of younger up-and-comers, elite credentials and pedigrees in traditional conservative ideology and instead leaning toward unapologetically combative, MAGA-friendly nominees. This suggested a move toward more explicitly political appointments, though the underlying conservative judicial philosophy remained constant.

The long-term implications of Trump's judicial legacy cannot be overstated. And every current Republican-appointed member of the court is affiliated with the Federalist Society. This means that Americans are likely to see justices affiliated with the Federalist Society advance the agenda of the conservative legal movement for decades to come. This transformation represented perhaps Trump's most enduring achievement, reshaping constitutional interpretation long after his presidency ended.

Religious Liberty and Traditional Values Protection

In the MAGA understanding of American history, religious faith wasn't just a private matter—it was the foundation upon which the entire American experiment was built. Trump's aggressive defense of religious liberty represented an effort to restore what conservatives saw as Christianity's rightful place in American public life, after decades of secularization and what they viewed as anti-religious discrimination.

The centerpiece of Trump's religious liberty agenda was the establishment of unprecedented institutional support for faith-based perspectives within the federal government. President Trump established the historic White House Faith Office – the first White House office focused exclusively on faith and located in the West Wing – reporting to the President and housed in the Domestic Policy Council. This wasn't merely symbolic—it represented a structural commitment to ensuring faith perspectives were integrated into policy-making at the highest levels.

The scope of Trump's religious liberty initiatives was comprehensive. President Trump created Centers for Faith with Faith Directors or Faith Liaisons in every department and agency. President Trump established the Religious Liberty Commission to secure and promote religious liberty for Americans of all faiths. This represented an unprecedented effort to institutionalize religious considerations across the entire federal government.

Perhaps most controversially, Trump established the Task Force to Eradicate Anti-Christian Bias. The task force, officially known as the Task Force to Eradicate Anti-Christian Bias, will be comprised of members of President Trump's cabinet and key government agencies. The task force will review the activities of all departments and agencies to identify and eliminate anti-Christian policies, practices, or conduct. This initiative reflected Trump's belief that Christians faced systematic discrimination in American society that required active government intervention to address.

The task force's mandate was sweeping. The task force will gather input from various stakeholders to ensure broad perspectives are considered, including faith-based organizations, State, local, and Tribal governments, and Americans affected by anti-Christian conduct. It will identify and address gaps in laws and enforcement that have contributed to anti-Christian conduct, including by remedying any failures to fully enforce the law against acts of anti-Christian hostility, vandalism, and violence.

Trump's approach to religious liberty was grounded in specific grievances against what conservatives saw as secular overreach. The Biden Department of Justice brought felony charges and obtained multi-year prison sentences against nearly two dozen pro-life Christians for praying and peacefully demonstrating outside abortion facilities. The Biden Department of Justice ignored hundreds of attacks on Catholic churches, charities, and pro-life centers. In Trump's first week back in office, he pardoned these pro-life activists, sending a clear message about his administration's priorities.

The religious liberty agenda extended into education policy as well. President Trump issued an executive order on school choice, supporting parents' rights to choose private, religious, or public charter schools for their children. President Trump ensured the One Big Beautiful Bill established the first national school choice program in American history, including for faith-based schools. This represented a fundamental challenge to the secular monopoly on public education that conservatives had long opposed.

Trump's rhetoric on religious liberty was characteristically bold. "To have a great nation, you have to have religion. I believe that so strongly. There has to be something after we go through all of this — and that something is God," President Trump highlighted the importance of faith in God. This wasn't just personal belief—it was a statement of governing philosophy that saw religious faith as essential to American greatness.

The approach also included direct challenges to church-state separation doctrines that conservatives viewed as hostile to religious expression. Trump said of the concept of church-state separation, "Let's forget about that for once." The administration green-lit political endorsements from the pulpit by effectively neutralizing enforcement of the Johnson Amendment, which traditionally prevented churches from making political endorsements while maintaining tax-exempt status.

Critics argued that Trump's religious liberty agenda represented an unconstitutional establishment of religion that privileged Christianity over other faiths and over secular perspectives. Therefore, we insist that religious freedom must include everyone, not only the select few. While this effort may appear to address certain forms of stigma against Christians, particularly against Catholics, in reality it weaponizes a certain understanding of religious freedom to legitimize discrimination against marginalized groups.

However, supporters saw Trump's approach as necessary correction of decades of anti-religious bias in American institutions. They argued that true religious liberty required active protection of religious perspectives in public life, not merely tolerance of private belief. In their view, the secular left had used concepts like "separation of church and state" to systematically exclude religious voices from public discourse, creating a de facto establishment of secular humanism.

The culmination of this approach was Trump's "America Prays" initiative, which represented an attempt to restore public recognition of America's religious heritage. President Trump reaffirmed our nation's founding principles: "When faith gets weaker, our country seems to get weaker. When faith gets stronger… good things happen for our country. It's amazing the way it seems to work that way. Under the Trump Administration, we're defending our rights and restoring our identity as a nation under God."

The Constitutional Vision

These four pillars of Trump's approach to law, order, and constitutional values—police support, gun rights, judicial conservatism, and religious liberty—weren't disconnected policy positions but components of a comprehensive vision of American governance. At its core, this vision rested on the belief that America's founding principles had been systematically undermined by liberal elites who sought to transform the country according to their own ideological preferences.

In the MAGA understanding, the Constitution wasn't a "living document" to be reinterpreted by each generation, but a fixed charter that established permanent principles of limited government, individual rights, and local control. The role of government wasn't to engineer social outcomes but to protect the conditions within which free people could pursue their own vision of the good life.

This constitutional philosophy had profound implications for contemporary debates. On policing, it meant supporting law enforcement officers who upheld the rule of law against chaos and criminality. On guns, it meant recognizing that the right to bear arms was fundamental to free citizenship, not subject to the whims of temporary political majorities. On courts, it meant appointing judges who would interpret law rather than make it, restoring democratic accountability to American governance. On religion, it meant acknowledging the historical and contemporary role of faith in American life, rather than treating religious belief as a private eccentricity to be marginalized from public discourse.

The MAGA constitutional vision represented both a reaction to decades of liberal governance and a positive program for American renewal. Its supporters argued that by returning to founding principles, America could recapture the dynamism and unity that had made it great. Its critics warned that this approach threatened pluralism, equality, and democratic norms that had evolved to include previously marginalized groups.

What seemed clear was that Trump's approach to constitutional interpretation had fundamentally altered American political discourse. Whether one agreed with his specific policies or not, his presidency demonstrated that constitutional principles could be powerful political tools, capable of mobilizing mass movements and reshaping institutions. The MAGA movement's success in framing contemporary debates in constitutional terms—from religious liberty to gun rights to judicial philosophy—showed the enduring power of America's founding documents to inspire and direct political action.

The ultimate test of this constitutional vision would be whether it could deliver on its promises of renewed prosperity, security, and national unity. But regardless of the outcomes, Trump's approach to law, order, and constitutional values had already achieved something significant: it had reminded Americans that their founding principles were not museum pieces but living guides to governance that retained the power to inspire dramatic change. In doing so, it had restored constitutional interpretation to the center of American political life, where the founders had always intended it to remain.

CHAPTER 8: CULTURAL WARS AND IDENTITY POLITICS

In the theater of American politics, few battles have been as visceral or as consequential as the cultural wars that defined the Trump era. What began as discrete policy disagreements—over education curricula, entertainment content, and religious expression—evolved into something far more profound: a fundamental clash over who gets to define American identity in the 21st century. For millions of Americans who rallied behind the MAGA banner, these weren't merely political skirmishes but existential struggles to preserve the values, traditions, and ways of life they saw under relentless assault from liberal elites who seemed intent on remaking America according to their own ideological vision.

The cultural wars of the Trump era represented more than politics as usual—they embodied a comprehensive worldview that saw American greatness rooted in traditional institutions, time-tested values, and shared cultural norms that had guided the nation for generations. From the classroom to the football field, from Hollywood studios to church sanctuaries, Trump supporters found themselves defending territory they believed was rightfully theirs against what they perceived as a coordinated campaign to marginalize their voices, delegitimize their beliefs, and fundamentally transform their country. What emerged wasn't just a political movement but a cultural counterrevolution that would reshape American discourse for years to come.

Traditional Family Values in a Changing Society

At the heart of the MAGA cultural worldview lay an unwavering commitment to what supporters called "traditional family values"—a constellation of beliefs about marriage, parenting, gender roles, and social organization that they argued had formed the bedrock of American civilization. Yet by the time Donald Trump emerged as their unlikely champion, these values seemed under siege from multiple directions: changing demographics, evolving social norms, new legal frameworks, and what conservatives saw as a deliberate campaign by progressive elites to deconstruct the nuclear family.

The MAGA movement's approach to family values represented something of a paradox. President Donald Trump, despite being twice divorced with five children by three women, has championed traditional family values. "We will again stand proudly for families and for life," Trump told anti-abortion protesters at the March For Life back in January. Critics pointed to this apparent contradiction, arguing that Trump's personal life hardly embodied the values he claimed to champion. But for his supporters, Trump's past mattered less than his present commitment to defending the institutional framework within which strong families could flourish.

The MAGA vision of family values wasn't merely nostalgic—it was actively defensive. The MAGA movement aligns closely with conservative values on social issues. Proponents champion traditional family values, oppose abortion rights, and advocate for stricter interpretations of religious freedoms. This social conservatism has drawn significant support from religious and socially conservative voters. This defensive posture reflected genuine concerns about rapid social change and its impact on family stability.

Central to this worldview was the belief that the traditional nuclear family—comprising a married mother and father raising their biological children—represented the optimal environment for child-rearing and social stability. PRESERVING SANCTITY OF LIFE: President Donald J. Trump's policies are ending taxpayer support of the abortion industry. This wasn't merely policy preference but moral conviction rooted in both religious teaching and sociological observation.

The movement's family values agenda extended beyond rhetoric into concrete policy initiatives. Trump's policies consistently supported what he termed the "sanctity of marriage" and the "foundational role of families." Republicans will promote a Culture that values the Sanctity of Marriage, the blessings of childhood, the foundational role of families, and supports working parents. These weren't empty slogans but reflected a comprehensive vision of social organization that prioritized family stability over individual autonomy when the two came into conflict.

However, the reality was more complex than the rhetoric sometimes suggested. Instead of fiscal responsibility and a focus on family values, we're seeing fiscal profligacy, policy decisions that could destabilize families, and political figures displaying a disregard for norms and decency in their personal lives. MAGA leaders have lost the vision on what "good" even looks like for families. Critics argued that Trump's policies, particularly on immigration, often worked against family unity, while his personal conduct seemed to contradict traditional moral teachings.

The immigration debate particularly highlighted these tensions. Despite the fact that refugee children and their families are often victims of rape, violence, and homicide, they are the ones being treated as criminals by enforcement policies that tear families apart, harm children, and facilitate the immediate removal and deportation without regard to asylum claims. The policy of family separation at the border created a stark contradiction between the movement's stated commitment to family values and its immigration enforcement priorities.

Yet for many MAGA supporters, these criticisms missed the larger point. Their concern wasn't hypocrisy but cultural survival. They saw traditional family structures under attack from multiple directions: economic policies that made single-income households impossible, educational systems that undermined parental authority, entertainment media that normalized alternative family arrangements, and legal frameworks that redefined marriage and gender. In this context, Trump's personal failings seemed less important than his willingness to use presidential power to defend traditional institutions.

The movement's approach to family values also reflected broader anxieties about social change and cultural displacement. "Joe Biden is the candidate of these privileged liberal hypocrites who hold you and your values in disdain," Trump declared to enthusiastic crowds. This wasn't just political rhetoric—it captured genuine feelings of cultural marginalization among Americans who felt their values were being systematically devalued by elite institutions.

This sense of cultural siege manifested in specific policy priorities that went beyond traditional conservative concerns. MAGA supporters didn't just want government to stay out of family affairs—they wanted active government intervention to protect families from what they saw as destructive social forces. This included restrictions on content in schools and media, support for religious exemptions from anti-discrimination laws, and policies that privileged married couples and traditional gender roles.

The evolution of Republican family policy during the Trump era reflected this shift from passive conservatism to active cultural defense. Most American parents (78 percent) believe that their children are going to inherit a worse future—the highest share in 30 years. Amid that uncertainty, they deserve a thoughtful plan. This parental anxiety drove much of the cultural warfare that would define the movement, particularly in education.

Education Battles: From Common Core to Critical Race Theory

No battleground in the cultural wars proved more contentious than America's classrooms, where MAGA supporters saw their children being exposed to what they viewed as radical ideologies designed to undermine traditional values and American patriotism. The education battles of the Trump era weren't merely about curriculum—they represented a fundamental struggle over who controls the narrative that shapes young American minds and what version of American history and values should be transmitted to the next generation.

The fight began even before Trump took office, with grassroots opposition to Common Core academic standards morphing into broader skepticism about federal involvement in education. But it was the emergence of Critical Race Theory as a political issue that turned local school board meetings into ideological battlegrounds and made education policy a central focus of the MAGA movement's cultural agenda.

Trump's approach to education reflected a conviction that American schools had become laboratories for left-wing indoctrination rather than institutions of learning. President Trump is ordering U.S. schools to stop teaching what he views as "critical race theory" and other material dealing with race and sexuality or risk losing their federal money. This wasn't merely policy preference but represented a comprehensive worldview that saw progressive educators as actively hostile to American values and traditions.

The scope of Trump's education agenda was sweeping. "On day one, I will sign a new executive order to cut federal funding for any school pushing critical race theory, transgender insanity, and other inappropriate racial, sexual, or political content on our children," Trump said previously. This language reflected the movement's belief that schools had moved far beyond traditional education into explicit political advocacy.

Critical Race Theory became the focal point of these battles, even though critical race theory is not usually taught in K-12 public schools to begin with. "It's not really even in the curriculum. People don't really engage critical race theory until graduate school and some undergraduate programs". But for MAGA supporters, the specific academic theory mattered less than what they saw as its practical manifestations in classroom discussions about race, privilege, and American history.

The breadth of the anti-CRT movement was remarkable. Although President Joe Biden has since revoked Trump's executive order, today the number of efforts to ban critical race theory has grown to 619, according to our database – CRT Forward – which was formally launched in 2021. This represented an unprecedented grassroots mobilization around education policy, with anti-CRT measures have been introduced in 49 states.

The political impact was immediate and substantial. Since January 2021, 14 states have passed into law what's popularly referred to as "anti-critical race theory" legislation. These laws and orders, combined with local actions to restrict certain types of instruction, now impact more than one out of every three children in the country. This represented a fundamental shift in how Americans approached education policy, from a bipartisan consensus supporting local control to active partisan intervention in curriculum decisions.

For MAGA supporters, these battles weren't about restricting education but about restoring it to its proper purpose. They argued that schools had been captured by progressive ideologues who were more interested in political indoctrination than academic instruction. "Getting critical race theory out of our schools is not just a matter of values, it's also a matter of national survival," Donald Trump railed at a rally. "We have no choice, the fate of any nation ultimately depends upon the willingness of its citizens to lay down — and they must do this — lay down their very lives to defend their country".

The movement's approach to education reform went beyond mere restriction of controversial content. The White House on Wednesday also reinstated an order from Mr. Trump's first term establishing the 1776 Commission to promote "patriotic education" in U.S. schools. This represented a positive vision of what American education should accomplish: instilling love of country, respect for founding principles, and pride in national achievements.

Critics argued that this approach would sanitize American history and prevent honest discussion of the nation's challenges. We live in an era of post-truth schooling, where historical realities have been outlawed and young people are being trained to accept that those who present honest accounts of the past should be punished. But MAGA supporters countered that their children were already receiving sanitized history—just sanitized in the opposite direction, emphasizing America's failures while ignoring its triumphs.

The practical impact on classroom instruction was significant. Local pressures against "critical race theory" have led to educators self-censoring, districts abandoning equity initiatives, and equity officers receiving threats. This created an atmosphere where teachers became cautious about discussing controversial topics, potentially limiting the kind of robust academic discourse that education should foster.

Yet from the MAGA perspective, this caution was appropriate. They argued that public schools, funded by taxpayer money, shouldn't be platforms for political advocacy of any kind. If teachers wanted to discuss controversial topics, they needed to do so in ways that respected the values and beliefs of all students and families, not just those aligned with progressive ideology.

The education battles also reflected broader concerns about parental authority. "Parents' rights" has taken off as an issue for Republican legislators over the past year, as families demanded greater input into what their children learned and how they learned it. This wasn't merely about content but about who ultimately had responsibility for shaping young minds: parents or professional educators.

The movement's success in mobilizing around education issues demonstrated the political power of parental anxiety. "A lot of students expressed really wanting to feel like their teachers care about them as people, not just as students. I believe you can't really care about a person unless you take their full identity into account," said one teacher, noting that most of her students were Black. "We're basically saying that students are not allowed to learn in the context of themselves". This highlighted the real tension at the heart of these battles: between educators who believed in acknowledging students' diverse backgrounds and experiences, and parents who worried that such acknowledgment might come at the expense of shared American identity.

Hollywood, Sports, and Entertainment Industry Conflicts

The entertainment industry became an unexpected battlefield in the cultural wars, as MAGA supporters found themselves increasingly alienated from an Hollywood establishment they viewed as contemptuous of their values and hostile to their political preferences. What emerged wasn't merely political disagreement but a comprehensive critique of how cultural elites used their platforms to promote progressive ideology while marginalizing conservative perspectives.

Trump's relationship with Hollywood was particularly complex, given his own entertainment background. No president has ever relied as much on the operating principles of the entertainment business. And none has ever had such a fraught relationship with it. This paradox captured the broader MAGA movement's relationship with popular culture: simultaneously influenced by it and critical of it.

The scope of Trump's criticism was comprehensive. Trump wrote on Truth Social: "Our great West Point (getting greater all the time!) has smartly cancelled the Award Ceremony for actor Tom Hanks. Important move! We don't need destructive, WOKE recipients getting our cherished American Awards!!! Hopefully the Academy Awards, and other Fake Award Shows, will review their Standards and Practices in the name of Fairness and Justice". This wasn't isolated criticism but part of a systematic challenge to Hollywood's cultural authority.

The entertainment industry found itself adapting to political pressure in ways it hadn't experienced since the McCarthy era. Trump and Republicans like Florida Gov. Ron DeSantis have repeatedly pushed back on "woke culture" as a core part of their political strategy. This created genuine economic concerns for an industry dependent on broad audience appeal.

The impact was measurable. Hollywood's biggest franchise plays and IP-driven films and shows – which is where it puts most of its money – are getting less diverse. "Look at the backlash to 'Little Mermaid' or 'Lord of the Rings,'" said a different top manager. "This is only going to increase post-election". Market forces were compelling changes that political pressure alone might not have achieved.

Some industry observers noted the shift in celebrity behavior. Eric Schiffer, CEO of Reputation Management Consultants, told Fox News Digital that "Hollywood learned the obvious – that attacking half the country is a dumb growth strategy and flattering is smart, scalable, and safe". This represented a significant change from the Trump-resistance rhetoric that had dominated Hollywood discourse during his first presidency.

The change was particularly notable among celebrities who had previously been critical of Trump. Rather than blast Trump by name, many of his celebrity critics are instead zipping their lips when it comes to mentioning the 47th president. This shift suggested that market considerations were overriding political preferences for at least some entertainment figures.

However, resistance remained strong among certain segments of the industry. Actress and climate change activist Jane Fonda took veiled jabs at President Donald Trump in a politically charged speech at the 31st annual Screen Actors Guild (SAG) Awards Sunday night and rallied Hollywood to stand up to the new administration. Fonda's approach—criticizing Trump without naming him—reflected the industry's awkward position between political conviction and economic pragmatism.

The sports world presented similar dynamics, though the conflicts there were even more public and divisive. The NFL's national anthem protests, initiated by Colin Kaepernick, became a defining cultural battleground that perfectly encapsulated the broader tensions between progressive activism and traditional patriotism.

Trump's involvement in the NFL controversy was immediate and aggressive. During a rally in Alabama, Trump dials up the anti-protests rhetoric by several notches, openly calling for team owners to fire players who demonstrate during the national anthem. "Wouldn't you love to see one of these NFL owners, when somebody disrespects our flag, to say, 'Get that son of a b**** off the field right now. Out! He's fired. He's fired'". This wasn't subtle political positioning but direct confrontation with the league and its players.

The impact was significant and immediate. This may very well go down in history as the season that changed football. The President of the United States declared a political war on some of the most visible players. And he wouldn't let it go. Trump's sustained attention to the issue elevated what might have been a limited protest into a national political controversy.

The protests themselves had begun as a specific response to police brutality. The protests began in the National Football League (NFL) after San Francisco 49ers quarterback Colin Kaepernick sat and later knelt during the anthem, before his team's preseason games of 2016. But Trump's intervention transformed the meaning of the protests in the public consciousness, making them as much about patriotism and respect for national symbols as about racial justice.

The political implications were substantial. Republican strategists and campaign staff tell BuzzFeed News that they see opportunities for candidates to make the NFL protests a political liability for Democrats defending seats in states President Donald Trump won in 2016. The issue provided a perfect wedge to separate Trump supporters from urban liberals and African American Democrats.

The divide was stark and largely predictable. Polling on the protests shows a huge racial and partisan divide, with a majority of Democrats and black voters saying it is appropriate for players to kneel, and a majority of Republicans and white voters saying it is inappropriate. This highlighted how the same action could be interpreted as either patriotic dissent or unpatriotic disrespect, depending on one's political and cultural perspective.

For MAGA supporters, the protests represented everything they disliked about contemporary elite culture: wealthy celebrities using their platforms to criticize America, progressive activists turning beloved traditions into political statements, and cultural institutions prioritizing ideology over entertainment. The fact that the protests occurred during the national anthem—a moment of shared patriotic ritual—made them particularly offensive to people who saw such rituals as essential to national unity.

The economic impact was real but complex. George Popson, a Republican from Texas, has always been a football fan, but this season he boycotted the NFL and he says it's all because of Donald Trump. Conservative boycotts did affect viewership, though the causes of declining NFL ratings were multifaceted and couldn't be attributed solely to political controversy.

The resolution of these conflicts remained uncertain. You can't argue that players can do the Trump celebration but don't have the right to make other political statements, including kneeling for the anthem. The principle of allowing political expression in sports seemed to work both ways, though the reception of different types of expression varied dramatically based on their political content.

The Role of Christianity in American Public Life

Perhaps no aspect of the cultural wars was more fundamental to the MAGA worldview than the proper role of Christianity in American society. For millions of Trump supporters, the United States wasn't merely a nation that happened to have many Christians—it was a fundamentally Christian nation whose founding principles, moral framework, and cultural traditions were inextricably linked to biblical faith. Yet by the Trump era, they saw this Christian heritage under systematic assault from secular elites who sought to privatize faith and eliminate its influence from public discourse.

Trump's approach to Christianity in public life represented a dramatic departure from the careful church-state balance that had characterized previous administrations. President Trump highlighted the importance of faith in God: "To have a great nation, you have to have religion. I believe that so strongly. There has to be something after we go through all of this — and that something is God." This wasn't diplomatic acknowledgment of religious diversity but explicit affirmation of faith's central role in national life.

The institutional changes Trump implemented reflected this conviction. President Trump established the historic White House Faith Office – the first White House office focused exclusively on faith and located in the West Wing – reporting to the President and housed in the Domestic Policy Council. This represented unprecedented formal recognition of religious perspectives in federal policymaking, signaling that faith considerations would be integral to governance rather than peripheral concerns.

The scope of Trump's religious liberty agenda was comprehensive. President Trump created Centers for Faith with Faith Directors or Faith Liaisons in every department and agency. President Trump established the Religious Liberty Commission to secure and promote religious liberty for Americans of all faiths. This systematic integration of religious perspectives across government represented a fundamental shift from previous approaches that had emphasized secular neutrality in public administration.

Most controversially, Trump established the Task Force to Eradicate Anti-Christian Bias, which he argued was necessary to address systematic discrimination against Christians in American society. The Biden Department of Justice brought felony charges and obtained multi-year prison sentences against nearly two dozen pro-life Christians for praying and peacefully demonstrating outside abortion facilities. The Biden Department of Justice ignored hundreds of attacks on Catholic churches, charities, and pro-life centers. For Trump supporters, this demonstrated clear anti-Christian bias that required active government intervention to correct.

The task force's mandate was sweeping. The task force will review the activities of all departments and agencies to identify and eliminate anti-Christian policies, practices, or conduct. It will identify and address gaps in laws and enforcement that have contributed to anti-Christian conduct, including by remedying any failures to fully enforce the law against acts of anti-Christian hostility, vandalism, and violence. This represented perhaps the most explicit government defense of Christian interests in modern American history.

Trump's rhetoric on Christianity was characteristically bold and uncompromising. At a Museum of the Bible event, Trump said of the concept of church-state separation, "Let's forget about that for once." President Trump reaffirmed our nation's founding principles: "When faith gets weaker, our country seems to get weaker. When faith gets stronger… good things happen for our country. It's amazing the way it seems to work that way. Under the Trump Administration, we're defending our rights and restoring our identity as a nation under God."

The practical implications extended into education policy, where Trump challenged decades of secular orthodoxy. "For most of our country's history, the bible was found in every classroom in the nation, yet in many schools today, students are instead indoctrinated with anti-religious propaganda and some are punished for their religious beliefs. Very, very strongly punished." This historical claim, whether entirely accurate or not, reflected the movement's belief that American education had been systematically de-Christianized to the detriment of both academic quality and moral formation.

The administration also moved aggressively to protect religious expression in previously restricted contexts. The administration green-lit political endorsements from the pulpit by effectively neutralizing enforcement of the Johnson Amendment, which traditionally prevented churches from making political endorsements while maintaining tax-exempt status. This represented a significant expansion of churches' political role, allowing them to function more explicitly as political actors rather than merely religious institutions.

Critics argued that Trump's approach violated constitutional principles of religious neutrality and threatened the rights of non-Christians. Therefore, we insist that religious freedom must include everyone, not only the select few. While this effort may appear to address certain forms of stigma against Christians, particularly against Catholics, in reality it weaponizes a certain understanding of religious freedom to legitimize discrimination against marginalized groups. This criticism reflected genuine concerns about whether Trump's policies privileged Christianity over other faiths or over secular perspectives.

However, Trump supporters argued that true religious neutrality had never existed—the question was whether government would be implicitly secular or explicitly religious in its orientation. They contended that the previous "neutral" approach had actually been biased against religious perspectives, creating a de facto establishment of secular humanism that was just as ideologically driven as any religious establishment would be.

The culmination of Trump's Christian nationalism agenda was the "America Prays" initiative, which represented an explicit call for national spiritual renewal. This initiative invited Americans to "rededicate ourselves to one nation under God" and reflected Trump's belief that national greatness was ultimately dependent on spiritual foundations rather than merely material prosperity or political institutions.

The political impact of Trump's Christian agenda was substantial. This social conservatism has drawn significant support from religious and socially conservative voters, while also sparking tensions with those who champion progressive social change. The mobilization of Christian voters became a crucial component of the MAGA coalition, providing both electoral energy and ideological coherence to the movement.

Yet the relationship between Trump personally and Christian values remained complex. Critics repeatedly pointed to apparent contradictions between Trump's personal conduct and Christian teachings, noting his multiple marriages, business practices, and often harsh rhetoric toward opponents. But for many Christian supporters, Trump's personal failings were less important than his willingness to use presidential power to defend Christian interests and values in public life.

The Cultural Revolution's Legacy

The cultural wars of the Trump era represented far more than political disagreements—they constituted a comprehensive challenge to the liberal consensus that had dominated American elite institutions for decades. From family values to education, from entertainment to religious expression, MAGA supporters mounted a systematic campaign to reclaim cultural territory they believed had been wrongfully ceded to progressive activists and secular elites.

The scope of this cultural counterrevolution was unprecedented in modern American politics. Unlike previous conservative movements that had focused primarily on limiting government power, the MAGA approach involved actively using government authority to promote traditional values and restrict progressive ideology. This represented a fundamental shift in conservative strategy, from defensive to offensive cultural warfare.

The results were mixed but significant. In education, anti-CRT legislation changed classroom instruction across much of the country. In entertainment, market pressures forced Hollywood to reconsider its political messaging. In sports, protests diminished as leagues responded to economic and political pressure. In religious liberty, Christians gained new protections and public recognition for their faith.

Yet resistance remained strong, particularly in major metropolitan areas and elite institutions where progressive values retained dominance. The cultural wars thus contributed to the continuing polarization of American society, with different regions and communities increasingly living according to different cultural norms and values.

The ultimate significance of the MAGA cultural agenda lay not in its specific policy achievements but in its demonstration that culture and politics were inseparable. By treating questions of education, entertainment, and religious expression as political issues requiring government intervention, the movement fundamentally altered how Americans thought about the relationship between public and private life.

For MAGA supporters, this cultural activism represented necessary defense of traditional American values against progressive assault. For critics, it represented dangerous government overreach into areas that should remain private. But both sides agreed that the stakes were enormous: nothing less than the fundamental character of American civilization.

The cultural wars thus became both a symptom and a cause of America's deeper divisions. They reflected genuine differences in values and worldview that couldn't be easily reconciled through political compromise. Whether these conflicts would eventually resolve through victory by one side or the other, or through some new synthesis that transcended the current divisions, remained an open question as Trump's presidency continued to reshape American cultural and political life.

What seemed certain was that the cultural wars had permanently altered American politics, making questions of identity, values, and cultural authority central to political discourse in ways that previous generations might not have anticipated. In the MAGA understanding, making America great again required not just economic prosperity or military strength, but cultural renewal based on traditional values and institutions. Whether that vision would ultimately prevail remained the fundamental question underlying all other political debates.

CHAPTER 9: MEDIA, TRUTH, AND INFORMATION WARS

In the summer of 2016, a simple two-word phrase began appearing with increasing frequency across social media feeds, cable news programs, and political rallies: "fake news." What started as a descriptor for fabricated stories circulating online rapidly evolved into something far more consequential—a linguistic weapon that would reshape the American media landscape and fundamentally alter how millions of citizens relate to information itself. The emergence and widespread adoption of this term marked not just a semantic shift, but the beginning of what many scholars now recognize as a new phase in the ongoing battle for control over public discourse and democratic narrative.

The phenomenon of "fake news" and its relationship to the MAGA movement represents more than political messaging; it embodies a comprehensive challenge to traditional information gatekeepers and reflects deeper tensions about authority, trust, and truth in the digital age. This information warfare extends beyond mere skepticism toward mainstream media—it encompasses the creation of alternative information ecosystems, the strategic deployment of social media for political mobilization, and the fundamental contest over who gets to define reality for the American public. Understanding this transformation is crucial to comprehending not only the MAGA movement's communication strategies but also the broader evolution of American political discourse in the 21st century.

The Architecture of Media Distrust

Trust in traditional news media has been eroding for decades, with American confidence in journalism institutions declining from broad bipartisan support in the 1970s to dramatically polarized views by 2023, where just 11% of Republicans express trust in media compared to 58% of Democrats. However, the MAGA movement's relationship with media distrust represents something qualitatively different from this broader trend—it constitutes a systematic critique of what supporters view as a fundamentally corrupted information system.

The concept of "fake news" as deployed within MAGA circles operates on multiple levels simultaneously. At its most basic level, it serves as a label for stories deemed inaccurate or misleading. But more significantly, it functions as a conceptual framework that allows supporters to dismiss unfavorable coverage while maintaining their epistemic worldview intact. Current research indicates that 66% of U.S. consumers believe that 76% or more of news on social media is biased, while 60% globally say news organizations regularly report false stories. This widespread skepticism provides fertile ground for more sophisticated critiques of media institutions.

Within MAGA discourse, media distrust extends beyond questions of accuracy to challenge the fundamental legitimacy of traditional journalism's role as an intermediary between events and public understanding. The movement's critique suggests that mainstream media outlets don't simply get facts wrong occasionally—they systematically distort reality to serve elite interests hostile to ordinary Americans. This framing transforms media skepticism from a consumer choice into a form of political resistance.

The timing of this critique proved particularly potent. As the World Economic Forum's Global Risks Report 2024 highlights, disinformation is now considered the world's top risk in the next two years, with only 40% of people saying they consistently trust news. The MAGA movement's media critique emerged precisely when technological disruption, economic pressures on news organizations, and broader social fragmentation had already weakened traditional journalism's authority and reach.

Social Media as the New Political Battlefield

The transformation of social media from networking platforms into primary venues for political engagement represents perhaps the most significant change in American political communication since the advent of television. Social media has become the primary medium through which political campaigning occurs today, allowing candidates to micro-target specific demographics and communicate directly with voters while bypassing traditional media gatekeepers.

The MAGA movement's mastery of social media techniques proved crucial to its political success. Unlike traditional political communication, which relied on crafted messages delivered through established channels, social media enables real-time, unfiltered communication that can appear more authentic and immediate. The rush of presidential candidates to platforms like TikTok during the 2024 election cycle reflects this transformation, as political office-seekers seek new ways to interact with key voter bases despite national security concerns about platform ownership.

The mobilization potential of social media extends beyond campaign communication to encompass grassroots organization and community building. MAGA supporters developed sophisticated networks for sharing information, coordinating activities, and reinforcing group identity through shared narratives and symbols. Social media provides powerful tools for activism and civic engagement, allowing users to support causes, encourage voting, and share information about political participation with unprecedented reach and speed.

The strategic use of viral campaigning—through reposts, retweets, and new visual content—allows a single message to reach millions instantly at a fraction of traditional advertising costs. This democratization of message amplification particularly benefited movements like MAGA, which could leverage passionate supporter networks to achieve massive reach without proportional resource investments.

However, social media's role in political mobilization brings significant complications. Research shows that "horse race" coverage and game-frame journalism, while entertaining and easy to produce, can foster public cynicism and mistrust of candidates and the political process by portraying politics primarily in terms of winning and losing rather than public service. Social media amplifies these dynamics by encouraging engagement through conflict and controversy rather than substantive policy discussion.

The Echo Chamber Phenomenon and Alternative Media Ecosystems

The concept of "echo chambers"—environments where individuals encounter only information that confirms their existing beliefs—has become central to understanding contemporary political polarization. Research demonstrates that when people preferentially connect with those holding similar opinions, they create echo chambers that increasingly polarize everyone in the network, while diverse networks tend to moderate extreme positions.

Within the MAGA ecosystem, alternative media outlets emerged to serve audiences seeking information that aligned with their political perspectives while challenging mainstream media narratives. These platforms range from cable news channels and talk radio programs to online publications, podcasts, and social media influencers. Together, they constitute a parallel information infrastructure that can provide comprehensive coverage of events from perspectives often absent in traditional media.

Studies in the UK and several other countries show that most people maintain relatively diverse media diets, with only small minorities—often just a few percent—exclusively consuming news from partisan sources. However, for those who do inhabit these echo chambers, the effects can be profound. Experimental research demonstrates that partisan echo chambers increase both policy and affective polarization compared to mixed discussion groups, suggesting that homogeneous political environments intensify polarization.

The MAGA movement's alternative media ecosystem serves multiple functions beyond information provision. It creates spaces for community formation around shared values and grievances, provides platforms for movement leaders to communicate directly with supporters, and offers alternative interpretive frameworks for understanding current events. These outlets often focus on stories under-covered by mainstream media, particularly those highlighting concerns of rural, working-class, or traditional conservative Americans.

Research on social media polarization reveals that right-leaning users often form more densely connected echo chambers and remain more isolated from alternative viewpoints, while also being more vocal and active in producing and consuming political information. This pattern suggests that conservative alternative media ecosystems may be particularly effective at maintaining audience engagement and reinforcing group identity.

The algorithmic nature of social media platforms can inadvertently intensify these dynamics. When users curate their feeds by unfollowing sources they consider untrustworthy, they may unknowingly isolate themselves into polarized networks, creating "epistemic bubbles" that limit exposure to diverse perspectives.

The Battle for Narrative Control

Beyond questions of media bias or platform algorithms lies a more fundamental contest: the struggle to control dominant narratives about American society, politics, and identity. In our digital age, the formation of public opinion no longer relies on clear separation between information producers and consumers, but on blurred boundaries between different types of discourse, creating new opportunities for narrative manipulation.

The MAGA movement's approach to narrative warfare operates through several mechanisms. First, it challenges the authority of traditional narrative-setters by questioning their legitimacy, motives, and accuracy. Second, it offers alternative interpretive frameworks that recontextualize events and trends in ways that support movement goals and worldview. Third, it creates emotional resonance through storytelling that connects policy positions to personal experiences and cultural values.

The 2024 U.S. election underscored vulnerabilities in America's information environment, as foreign actors weaponized AI to deploy deepfakes and bot-driven campaigns aimed at stoking racial and economic tensions, while China's "Spamouflage Dragon" network specifically targeted American elections. This international dimension adds complexity to domestic information battles, as external actors seek to exploit existing divisions for their own strategic purposes.

The contest for narrative control extends beyond electoral politics to encompass broader cultural and social questions. MAGA supporters often frame their media criticism as defending ordinary Americans against elite manipulation—a narrative that resonates with broader populist themes about authentic versus artificial, grassroots versus astroturf, and real Americans versus cosmopolitan elites.

In modern conflict, controlling the narrative has become an essential element of warfare, with advanced tools enabling organizations and governments to secure influence within online landscapes through strategic messaging, digital propaganda, and media manipulation. The MAGA movement's sophisticated approach to narrative construction demonstrates understanding of these dynamics and their application to domestic political competition.

Contemporary analysis reveals that narrative control has become inseparable from broader strategies, as the ability to craft and sustain compelling stories is now as critical as physical actions in determining strategic success. This recognition explains the intense focus that MAGA leaders place on message discipline, alternative media development, and direct communication with supporters.

Information Warfare in the Digital Age

The convergence of technological capability, political polarization, and media fragmentation has created conditions for what scholars increasingly recognize as information warfare on the domestic front. AI-powered disinformation campaigns now leverage sophisticated techniques such as deepfake propaganda, bot-driven astroturfing, algorithmic amplification, and large-scale sentiment manipulation to manufacture false realities and disrupt political processes.

Within this environment, the MAGA movement's information strategies must be understood not merely as political communication but as participation in a broader contest for cognitive dominance. Recent statistics indicate that 62% of online content is now deemed false, with 86% of global citizens exposed to misinformation and 40% of social media content being fake. These conditions create both opportunities and challenges for movements seeking to establish alternative narratives.

The democratization of content creation and distribution through digital platforms means that traditional barriers to mass communication have largely dissolved. Anyone with internet access can potentially reach global audiences, create compelling multimedia content, and build substantial followings. This technological shift has enabled grassroots movements like MAGA to compete directly with established institutions for audience attention and narrative influence.

However, the same technologies that enable grassroots communication also facilitate manipulation by sophisticated actors. Research demonstrates that exposure to higher proportions of false news decreases trust in legitimate news while making people more overconfident in their ability to distinguish truth from falsehood. These findings suggest that information warfare tactics may be most effective precisely when they undermine general confidence in information quality rather than promoting specific false beliefs.

The Implications for Democratic Discourse

The transformation of media, truth, and information warfare within the MAGA movement reflects broader challenges facing democratic societies in the digital age. Studies show that exposure to misinformation is linked to lower trust in mainstream media across party lines, while also increasing trust in government when one's preferred party holds power. These patterns suggest that information consumption increasingly aligns with partisan identity rather than traditional journalistic standards.

The long-term implications of these trends remain uncertain. On one hand, the democratization of information creation and distribution enables previously marginalized voices to participate in public discourse and challenges institutional monopolies on truth-telling. On the other hand, the fragmentation of shared epistemic foundations threatens the common ground necessary for democratic deliberation and compromise.

Recent social media migrations, such as the movement from X to Bluesky following the 2024 election, raise concerns about further polarization as users self-sort into ideologically homogeneous platforms. These developments suggest that technical solutions alone may be insufficient to address the deeper social and political dynamics driving information fragmentation.

The MAGA movement's approach to media, truth, and information warfare thus represents both symptom and cause of broader transformations in American political communication. Its success in mobilizing supporters through alternative media ecosystems and narrative frameworks demonstrates the political potency of these strategies. However, the broader implications for democratic governance and social cohesion remain contested and evolving.

As American society continues navigating this transformed information landscape, understanding the MAGA movement's sophisticated approach to media criticism, alternative narrative construction, and digital mobilization becomes crucial for comprehending contemporary political dynamics. Whether these developments ultimately strengthen or weaken democratic institutions may depend on how successfully society adapts its norms, practices, and institutions to address the challenges and opportunities of the digital information age.

The battle for narrative control that characterized the MAGA movement's rise reflects deeper questions about authority, authenticity, and truth in democratic societies. These questions extend far beyond any single political movement to encompass fundamental issues about how democratic publics form opinions, make decisions, and maintain the shared understanding necessary for collective self-governance. The resolution of these tensions will likely shape American political discourse for generations to come.

CHAPTER 10: THE TWITTER PRESIDENCY AND DIRECT COMMUNICATION

On May 28, 2009, at 4:17 PM, Donald Trump sent his first tweet from the handle @realDonaldTrump: "Be sure to tune in and watch Donald Trump on Late Night with David Letterman as he presents the Top Ten List tonight!" What began as a straightforward promotional message would evolve into one of the most consequential communication experiments in American political history. Over nearly twelve years, Trump would tweet approximately 57,000 times, fundamentally altering the relationship between political leadership and public discourse. His Twitter feed became more than a communication tool—it transformed into a direct pipeline that bypassed traditional media gatekeepers, created new forms of political theater, and established a template for digital-age governance that continues to influence political communication worldwide.

The concept of a "Twitter presidency" encompasses far more than prolific social media use. It represents a fundamental reimagining of how political power communicates with democratic publics, how leaders construct and maintain their authority, and how modern movements mobilize supporters in the digital age. Trump's approach to direct communication—through social media platforms, massive rallies, meme warfare, and simplified messaging—created what scholars now recognize as a new paradigm in political leadership. This paradigm prioritizes immediacy over deliberation, emotional connection over institutional protocol, and theatrical impact over conventional diplomatic norms. Understanding this transformation is essential to comprehending both the MAGA movement's success and the broader evolution of democratic communication in the twenty-first century.

Breaking the Media Filter: The Direct Communication Revolution

The emergence of social media fundamentally changed how political communication takes place in the United States, but no figure exploited this transformation more effectively than Donald Trump. Traditional presidential communication had long relied on careful mediation—press conferences, prepared statements, and formal addresses filtered through journalistic interpretation and analysis. Trump used Twitter to bypass mainstream media by communicating with the public directly rather than using more traditional outlets, creating what communication scholars describe as an unprecedented level of unfiltered access between a political leader and mass audiences.

This strategy built upon a long presidential tradition of seeking direct communication with the American people. Presidents want to get their message out, unfiltered by the press, and in that sense, what Donald Trump is doing with social media is not new. Franklin D. Roosevelt's fireside chats, Ronald Reagan's prime-time addresses, and Barack Obama's early social media experimentation all represented efforts to circumvent traditional media interpretation. However, Trump's approach differed qualitatively in its frequency, spontaneity, and confrontational tone toward the media establishment itself.

The scale and impact of Trump's Twitter usage was extraordinary. Over nearly twelve years, Trump tweeted around 57,000 times, including about 8,000 times during the 2016 election campaign and over 25,000 times during his presidency. When Twitter permanently suspended his account in January 2021, @realDonaldTrump had over 88.9 million followers, representing one of the largest direct communication networks ever assembled by a political figure.

The strategic advantages of this approach proved significant. Through platforms such as social media, presidents can directly address the public, bypassing traditional media outlets. This has strengthened the president's ability to sell preferred agenda items directly to the public. Trump's tweets functioned as policy announcements, staff dismissal notifications, and diplomatic communications, fundamentally altering the traditional rhythm of government communication. Press secretaries found themselves responding to presidential communications they had not previewed, while foreign leaders monitored Twitter feeds for policy signals traditionally conveyed through diplomatic channels.

The confrontational aspect of Trump's media approach distinguished it from previous presidential communication strategies. The president-elect's choice to control his own public communication is driven, at least in part, by his open disdain for the mainstream media. Rather than simply seeking alternative channels, Trump actively attacked traditional media credibility while promoting his own direct communication as more trustworthy and authentic. This created a dynamic where his communication style became inseparable from his broader political message about establishment institutions and elite gatekeeping.

Rally Culture as Mass Mobilization Theater

Trump's mastery of direct communication extended far beyond social media into the physical realm of political rallies, which became central to his political brand and movement-building strategy. A Trump rally has the feel of an all-day pep rally mixed with a megachurch service — except with Trumpism as the religion. These events functioned as more than campaign stops; they served as community-building exercises, identity-formation experiences, and theatrical performances that reinforced movement solidarity.

The theatrical elements of Trump rallies were carefully orchestrated to maximize emotional impact and symbolic resonance. Critical theory scholar Douglas Kellner compares the elaborate staging used in Trump rallies with preparation of photo op sequences and aggressive hyping of huge attendance expected, noting how media coverage would cut between Trump's jet circling the stadium, rising crowd excitement, the motorcade arrival, and the triumphant entrance of the candidate presented as political savior.

Analysis of rally dynamics reveals sophisticated techniques for creating emotional connection and group identity. Analysis of Trump rallies shows how they functioned as 'morality plays' in which internal enemies (the press) and external enemies (protestors) were silenced, cowed and ejected as a result of Trump's agency, thereby showing how America could become great again. These performances allowed attendees to experience, in microcosm, the broader political transformation Trump promised for the nation.

The community aspect of Trump rallies proved particularly significant for movement building. The rallies are places where a movement largely defined by grievance can be together, away from opponents — not to mention assertions that Trump lies and is harmful to democracy. For supporters, these events provided spaces for affirming shared values, processing political anxieties, and experiencing collective identity in ways that online communication alone could not achieve.

The merchandising and cultural elements surrounding rallies contributed to their effectiveness as mobilization tools. People dress up for them in a way they don't for other politicians, with vendor networks creating "a growing sea of Trumpwear" that functioned as both economic opportunity and identity expression. The comparison to concert culture was deliberate and strategic: "It's kind of the same vibe. So I followed Dead & Company and Phish around all summer, and now I'm out here doing the same thing, but selling political merchandise".

Trump's campaign recognized the psychological impact of these gatherings and strategically leveraged them for broader political goals. To drive up turnout, Trump's campaign ran an unconventional ground game. He targeted irregular voters through community building, rather than traditional methods. Organizations supporting Trump used rallies not just for immediate political messaging but for creating longer-term community connections that could sustain political engagement beyond specific election cycles.

The rally format also served Trump's communication strengths by providing an environment optimized for his speaking style and audience interaction. Trump's messaging was simple, straightforward, and emotional, which analysts found engaged well with his "consumers"—voters. He appealed to their discontent over the economy, immigration, and national pride. The rally setting amplified these messages through crowd response, creating feedback loops that reinforced both speaker and audience engagement.

Meme Warfare and Digital Age Political Communication

The integration of meme culture into official government communication represents one of the most striking innovations of Trump's digital communication strategy. Since January, the Trump administration has shifted its tone on social media to cater to its MAGA base. Many posts — several of which play off of trending memes — appear to showcase aggression toward some longtime political targets. This approach transformed traditional government communication by incorporating viral internet culture, humor, and visual storytelling into official policy messaging.

The strategic deployment of memes serves multiple communication functions simultaneously. Memetic warfare is a modern type of information warfare and psychological warfare involving the propagation of memes on social media, representing what experts describe as "competition over narrative, ideas, and social control in a social-media battlefield". The Trump administration's adoption of these techniques elevated meme production from grassroots activity to official government strategy.

The technological sophistication of contemporary meme warfare has expanded dramatically with artificial intelligence capabilities. Sophisticated generative AI models have now taken meme production one step further. They offer a myriad of new possibilities "to create manipulated and fictional content to target political enemies". White House accounts have also shared AI-generated images of Trump as the pope, a "Star Wars" character and Superman, demonstrating how advanced tools enable rapid production of visually compelling content.

The administration's approach to meme communication deliberately challenged traditional governmental communication norms. Such posts have generated some shock online, which the White House itself appears to have referred to this month. In a post on X, the official account wrote: "Nowhere in the Constitution does it say we can't post banger memes". This self-aware acknowledgment of controversy demonstrated strategic understanding of how boundary-pushing content generates attention and engagement.

The effectiveness of this approach stems from its alignment with contemporary social media algorithms and user behavior. Social media has drastically changed since Trump's first term — when users would mainly see posts from accounts they followed. Now, many social media platforms use an individualized algorithm for each account that "privileges things that pop and that go viral". Understanding these algorithmic preferences allowed the administration to maximize reach and engagement through strategically provocative content.

The scale of memetic warfare operations extends far beyond individual posts to encompass coordinated campaigns and sustained narrative strategies. Memes have become ideal vehicles for a form of psychological and ideological warfare. Hence, the meme becomes the weapon, influencing public thought through humour, satire, or fear. This represents a fundamental shift in how governments engage in public communication, moving from traditional public relations to active participation in digital culture wars.

The global nature of contemporary meme warfare adds additional complexity to domestic political communication. Globally, memes are weaponised differently depending on political systems, reflecting unique socio-political goals. The Trump administration's embrace of these techniques both influenced and was influenced by international practices, creating new forms of political communication that blur boundaries between domestic governance and global information competition.

The Power of Simplified Messaging and Political Theater

Trump's communication effectiveness stems significantly from his mastery of simplified messaging techniques that prioritize emotional impact over complex policy explanation. Trump's rhetoric often frames complex issues in binary terms, using absolutes such as "always" and "never" to express uncompromising stances. This approach creates clear conceptual frameworks that audiences can easily understand and remember, even when addressing complicated political realities.

The linguistic characteristics of Trump's communication style have been extensively analyzed for their persuasive effectiveness. Trump's evocative and meaningful uses of pitch, amplitude, speech rate, rhythm, and other vocal measures combine to make his paralanguage exceptionally and counter-normatively informal. This informality serves strategic purposes by creating perceived authenticity and relatability that distinguishes him from conventional political figures.

Research demonstrates that Trump's communication approach provides significant advantages in contemporary political environments. A populist communication style – grandiose, dynamic, and informal – may have 'trumped' a carefully-reasoned platform. Analysis of primary campaign speeches showed that Trump scored highest on (a) grandiosity ratings, (b) use of first person pronouns, (c) greater pitch dynamics, and (d) informal communication compared to more experienced political competitors.

The strategic deployment of repetition amplifies the impact of simplified messages. Conventional wisdom in the advertising world is that it takes seven repetitions before a slogan or product feature starts to become memorable. Trump has no resistance to hammering the same message home – regardless of how accurate it is — at every opportunity. This technique ensures that key themes penetrate public consciousness even in crowded information environments.

Trump's use of memorable phrases and branding demonstrates sophisticated understanding of cognitive psychology and marketing principles. Trump also exercises the power of catch phrases. Going back to "You're fired!" during "The Apprentice" to today's use of "radical left lunatic" and "low IQ individual" in disparaging whatever political foe is on his radar at the moment. The creation of lasting labels like "Crooked Hillary" and "Crazy Kamala" illustrates how simplified messaging can shape long-term public perception of political figures.

The theatrical elements of Trump's communication extend beyond specific techniques to encompass his entire public persona. Trump has expanded his rhetorical field way beyond giving formal speeches standing behind a podium. His messaging turf includes social media, marathon rallies and impromptu give-and-take gaggles with reporters. This multi-platform approach creates consistent messaging across different contexts while maintaining the appearance of spontaneity and authenticity.

The psychological appeal of Trump's simplified messaging relates to broader patterns in contemporary political communication. The lure of 'Trump-speak' is rooted in the way it triggers voters' cognitive biases. By presenting complex realities through simplified frameworks, his communication approach reduces cognitive burden for audiences while providing clear emotional cues for political alignment.

The integration of entertainment values into political messaging represents another crucial aspect of Trump's theatrical approach. Recent studies frame his communication style as comedic and entertaining, polarizing, anti-intellectual and conversational. This entertainment orientation helps maintain audience attention in media environments characterized by information overload and shortened attention spans.

The Infrastructure of Direct Communication

The success of Trump's direct communication strategy required sophisticated technological and organizational infrastructure that extended far beyond individual social media accounts. Trump's administration will stay unfiltered, bold, and ready to take on the media—ensuring that his message is heard loud and clear, no matter the challenges ahead. With AI, social media, and virtual engagement tools at his disposal, Trump's second term will mark the next phase in the evolution of political communication in America.

The team responsible for managing this communication infrastructure operated with unprecedented freedom and creativity within government constraints. Administration officials said it is a relatively small team of roughly a dozen people that handles its social media presence, yet this compact group managed to generate massive engagement and influence across multiple platforms. The White House has held multiple "media row" days on campus, including bringing in conservative influencers last week to get out its message, demonstrating strategic integration of traditional and new media approaches.

The philosophical approach underlying this communication strategy explicitly rejected conventional governmental communication norms. "I would describe this team as the department of offense," White House deputy communications director Kaelan Dorr told The Hill in an interview. This offensive orientation prioritized message amplification and political combat over traditional public relations concerns about institutional dignity or diplomatic protocol.

The scalability and reach of this communication approach proved remarkable. A White House official said the administration's official social media accounts, including on Truth Social, have added over 16 million new followers across platforms since Inauguration Day. This growth demonstrates the continuing appeal of direct communication approaches even after Trump's initial novelty had worn off.

The integration of emerging technologies into official communication represented a significant innovation in governmental practice. With AI, social media analytics to ensure messages resonate with the right groups, allowing for targeted, effective outreach to key demographics, the administration leveraged technological capabilities that previous governments had not systematically employed for political messaging.

The broader implications of these communication innovations extend far beyond any single administration or political figure. President Obama was the first president to effectively harness the power of social media. Trump is the first president to use it to bypass the media and communicate directly with his base. This evolution represents a fundamental shift in the relationship between democratic governance and public communication that will likely influence political practice for decades to come.

The Democratization and Disruption of Political Communication

Trump's approach to direct communication has created both democratizing opportunities and disruptive challenges for American political discourse. Trump floods the rhetorical zone, grabbing and maintaining the public's attention with frequent social media posts the media can't wait to report and analyze. He is certainly the most accessible president for the news media in American history. This accessibility democratizes political communication by making leadership more immediately available to public observation and interaction.

However, this democratization comes with significant trade-offs in terms of traditional institutional norms and deliberative processes. The result is that the press feels like they have to fight for access and are more likely to frame their coverage in ways that give them access instead of ways that help the public. This dynamic fundamentally altered the traditional relationship between government and press, creating new forms of dependency and conflict.

The long-term implications of Trump's communication innovations remain contested and uncertain. No other president in American history has conducted public communication like Trump and it is unlikely any future president could duplicate his approach (which might be a good thing). Yet the techniques and expectations he established continue influencing political communication across the political spectrum.

The global impact of these communication strategies extends American political influence through digital platforms and cultural export. How he chooses to relate to each leader around the world will mirror his style that seemed to result in his election to the Presidency…frankness, deflection, rebuttal, decisiveness, relatability, as well as frequent and often communication. This communication approach became part of American soft power projection, influencing how other leaders and governments approach digital communication.

The educational and cautionary aspects of Trump's communication effectiveness offer lessons for democratic societies more broadly. We can borrow from the best elements of his style: he keeps his ideas simple and memorable; he knows his audience and addresses them directly; he appeals to their emotions. So sure, try this at home — but with caution!. Understanding these techniques becomes crucial for media literacy and democratic participation in digitally mediated political environments.

Conclusion: The Lasting Impact of the Twitter Presidency

The Twitter presidency represents more than a communication innovation—it constitutes a fundamental transformation in how democratic leadership operates in the digital age. Trump's approach to direct communication, rally culture, meme warfare, and simplified messaging created new templates for political engagement that transcend partisan boundaries. Whether viewed as democratic innovation or institutional disruption, these changes have permanently altered expectations for political communication and will continue influencing American governance long after specific administrations conclude.

The success of Trump's communication strategy demonstrates the continuing evolution of democratic practice in response to technological change. His ability to bypass traditional gatekeepers, create direct emotional connections with supporters, and maintain constant public engagement through multiple channels provided a competitive advantage that more conventional political figures struggled to match. Understanding these dynamics becomes essential for comprehending contemporary political competition and the future trajectory of democratic communication.

The broader implications of the Twitter presidency extend to fundamental questions about authority, authenticity, and institutional mediation in democratic societies. As political communication continues evolving through technological innovation, the techniques pioneered during Trump's presidency will likely influence how future leaders build public support, mobilize movements, and exercise democratic authority. The challenge for democratic societies lies in preserving the benefits of direct communication while maintaining institutional norms that support deliberative governance and social cohesion.

CHAPTER 11: THE ESTABLISHMENT STRIKES BACK

The morning after Donald Trump's 2016 electoral victory, Washington's political establishment awoke to a reality they had not anticipated and were not prepared to accept. The insurgent candidate who had spent months attacking the "swamp," deriding political elites, and promising to "drain" the very institutions that had long governed American democracy had somehow captured the presidency. What followed was not the typical honeymoon period between a new administration and the existing power structure, but rather an unprecedented confrontation between an outsider president and virtually every pillar of the American establishment. From Republican Party leaders struggling to maintain control of their own organization, to Democratic opposition mobilizing impeachment proceedings, to federal bureaucrats accused of "deep state" resistance, to grassroots social movements organizing mass protests—the traditional guardians of American institutional power launched a multifaceted campaign to contain, constrain, and ultimately defeat Trumpism.

This establishment response revealed fundamental tensions within American democracy about the relationship between popular sovereignty and institutional governance, between democratic mandates and constitutional constraints, and between political loyalty and professional duty. The conflict that emerged was not simply partisan—it cut across traditional party lines, ideological boundaries, and institutional divisions. Republican leaders found themselves torn between party loyalty and institutional preservation. Democratic politicians discovered the limits of conventional political opposition in an unconventional era. Federal bureaucrats faced impossible choices between presidential directives and professional ethics. And millions of Americans who had never considered themselves political activists suddenly found themselves part of a "resistance" movement. Understanding this multifaceted establishment response is crucial to comprehending both the MAGA movement's resilience and the broader transformation of American political discourse in the twenty-first century.

Republican Party: The Internal Civil War

The Trump presidency exposed deep fissures within the Republican Party that had been developing for decades, ultimately culminating in what The New York Times described as a "hostile takeover" and "a victory of right-wing populism over the old conservative establishment." The transformation was so complete that by Trump's second term, polling found that 53% of Republican voters saw loyalty to Trump as central to their political identity and what it means to be a Republican.

The roots of this internal division traced back to earlier factional conflicts. During the Barack Obama presidency, the Republican Party had experienced tension between its governing class (the Republican establishment) and the anti-establishment, small-government Tea Party movement. However, the Trump phenomenon represented something qualitatively different—not merely a policy disagreement but a fundamental challenge to the party's institutional structure, ideological coherence, and relationship with traditional conservative principles.

Trump's 2016 primary victory came despite, not because of, establishment support. The depletion of organizational capacity partly led to Trump's victory in the Republican primaries against the wishes of a very weak party establishment and traditional power brokers. This victory pattern established a template for how Trump would relate to party institutions throughout his presidency—as an external force that captured and redirected them rather than as a leader who rose through and embodied traditional party structures.

The establishment's resistance took multiple forms. Senate Republicans, particularly under the leadership of Mitch McConnell, attempted to serve as an internal check on Trump's more extreme impulses while simultaneously supporting much of his policy agenda. McConnell was described as the last powerful member of the Republican establishment, with his retirement marking its end. The tension between institutional loyalty and personal loyalty to Trump created ongoing conflicts that ultimately resolved in Trump's favor.

By 2021, analysis revealed distinct Republican factions emerging from the Trump experience: Never Trumpers (including figures like Bill Kristol and Senator Mitt Romney), Sometimes Trumpers (including McConnell and former UN Ambassador Nikki Haley), and Always Trumpers (including Senators Ted Cruz and Josh Hawley). However, these distinctions proved temporary as Trump's control over the party base forced even skeptical Republicans into accommodation or retirement.

The most dramatic manifestation of this internal struggle occurred around the January 6, 2021 Capitol attack and its aftermath. Republicans in Congress faced a choice between accountability (supporting impeachment or other disciplinary measures) and party unity (defending Trump despite their private reservations). The vast majority chose party unity, revealing the extent to which Trump's personal brand had become synonymous with Republican identity for the party's base voters.

Research during Trump's second term revealed the thoroughness of his victory within Republican ranks. During Trump's second presidency, Republican members of Congress were described by The New Republic magazine as submissive to Trump, letting him dictate policies without pushback. The few remaining establishment Republicans found themselves politically isolated, with limited influence over party direction or policy priorities.

Democratic Opposition: The Limits of Constitutional Resistance

The Democratic Party's response to Trump represented the most sustained opposition effort by a major political party against a sitting president in modern American history. However, this opposition revealed significant constraints on what legislative minorities can accomplish against a determined executive, particularly when that executive maintains strong support from their party base and controls key governmental institutions.

The impeachment strategy became the centerpiece of Democratic resistance, with the House of Representatives ultimately impeaching Trump twice—first over the Ukraine scandal and second over the January 6 Capitol attack. Speaker of the House Nancy Pelosi initially resisted calls for impeachment, but events forced her hand as evidence of presidential misconduct accumulated and pressure from the Democratic base intensified.

The first impeachment, launched on September 24, 2019, focused on Trump's efforts to pressure Ukraine into investigating Joe Biden in exchange for military aid. Despite extensive hearings and evidence gathering, the process revealed the limitations of impeachment as a constraint on presidential power when the president's party controls the Senate. The Trump administration's strategy of non-cooperation—asserting executive privilege and refusing to honor congressional subpoenas—demonstrated how presidents can frustrate congressional oversight even during formal impeachment proceedings.

The second impeachment, following the January 6 attack, proceeded more rapidly but faced similar structural constraints. While the House successfully passed articles of impeachment with bipartisan support (including ten Republican votes), the Senate trial again ended in acquittal. The constitutional requirement for a two-thirds Senate majority for conviction meant that impeachment remained largely a symbolic gesture rather than an effective constraint on presidential behavior.

Democratic opposition efforts extended beyond impeachment to encompass a broad range of investigative, legislative, and judicial strategies. The party used its House majority after 2018 to conduct extensive oversight hearings, issue subpoenas for administration officials and documents, and maintain constant pressure on the Trump administration through media coverage of its investigations.

However, these efforts often encountered the same obstacles that limited impeachment's effectiveness. The Trump administration's blanket refusal to cooperate with congressional oversight, combined with lengthy court battles over executive privilege claims, meant that much Democratic investigative work occurred too slowly to influence public opinion or policy outcomes in real time.

The 2024 election outcome and Trump's return to power forced Democrats to confront the limitations of their resistance strategy. Despite four years of investigation, two impeachments, and multiple criminal indictments, Trump maintained sufficient popular support to regain the presidency. This outcome prompted soul-searching within Democratic ranks about whether their constitutional resistance approach had been effective or whether alternative strategies might have been more successful.

Current Democratic responses to Trump's second term reflect lessons learned from the first experience. Party leaders have generally discouraged new impeachment efforts, recognizing their limited effectiveness when Republicans control both chambers of Congress. Instead, Democrats have focused on state-level resistance, judicial challenges, and grassroots organizing as more promising avenues for opposition.

Deep State Theories and Bureaucratic Reality

Perhaps no aspect of the establishment response to Trump generated more controversy than the role of federal bureaucrats and the allegations of "deep state" resistance that surrounded their actions. Trump's supporters used the term deep state to refer to allegations that intelligence officers and executive branch officials were influencing policy via leaks or other internal means, while critics argued that such claims represented conspiracy theories designed to delegitimize legitimate institutional constraints on presidential power.

The concept gained prominence early in Trump's presidency when his chief strategist Stephen Bannon described the administration's daily battle for "deconstruction of the administrative state." This framing positioned career federal employees not as neutral implementers of policy but as potential obstacles to the Trump agenda who needed to be overcome or removed.

Trump's own rhetoric reinforced this narrative. During his 2024 campaign, he used the concept of the "deep state" to rally support, portraying it as a shadowy network of bureaucrats and officials working against his agenda. He frequently vowed to "demolish the deep state," outlining a multi-step plan to gut the civil service, limit institutional power, and replace career officials with loyalists.

The reality of bureaucratic resistance proved more complex than either the "deep state" conspiracy theory or its complete dismissal suggested. Career bureaucrats did engage in various forms of resistance to Trump administration policies, ranging from leaking information to the press, to slow-walking implementation of controversial directives, to refusing to participate in policies they viewed as illegal or unethical.

However, research on this resistance revealed it was neither coordinated nor particularly effective. One of the chief lessons Trump learned from his first administration was that senior career bureaucrats, left to their own devices, were willing and able to sabotage him through various forms of institutional resistance. Examples included FBI officials' handling of the Russia investigation, CDC officials' resistance to COVID-19 messaging directives, and USAID bureaucrats' concealment of programs they feared Trump would terminate.

The "deep state" narrative proved politically useful for Trump even when the underlying resistance was limited. Survey research showed that a March 2018 poll by Monmouth University found most respondents (63%) were unfamiliar with "deep state" but a majority believe that a deep state likely exists in the United States when described as "a group of unelected government and military officials who secretly manipulate or direct national policy."

Scholarly analysis suggested that the United States does not have a deep state in the traditional sense because American bureaucracy is relatively weak compared to other democracies. Federal agencies are very much under the thumb of elected presidents and their politically appointed administrators. The chronically underfunded, understaffed federal bureaucracy lacks the institutional autonomy that characterizes deep states in other political systems.

Nevertheless, the perception of bureaucratic resistance had real political consequences. It provided justification for Trump's efforts to expand presidential control over the civil service through mechanisms like Schedule F reclassification, which would make tens of thousands of federal jobs subject to political appointment rather than merit-based hiring and firing protections.

Social Movements and Counter-Narratives

The Trump presidency sparked the largest and most sustained social movement opposition to a sitting president in modern American history. These movements, collectively known as "the resistance," encompassed a diverse array of organizations, tactics, and constituencies united by opposition to Trump's policies and governing style.

The movement's origins traced to the immediate aftermath of Trump's 2016 victory, when a Facebook event titled "Trump is Not My President" received over 40,000 interactions within days of the election. This early online organizing foreshadowed the role social media would play in coordinating opposition activities throughout Trump's presidency.

The Women's March on January 21, 2017, established the template for large-scale resistance activities. Drawing millions of participants worldwide, the march demonstrated both the scale of anti-Trump sentiment and the organizational capacity of opposition groups. The event's success led to the formation of ongoing organizations like Indivisible, which grew from a viral Google Doc about confronting elected officials into an organization with over 4,000 affiliated local groups by 2021.

Social media played a crucial role in amplifying resistance messages and coordinating activities. The #Resist hashtag became one of the most consistent symbols of anti-Trump activism, appearing in over 2.5

million tweets in the three days following Trump's initial Muslim ban announcement. The hashtag #NotMyPresident also gained widespread use, though it drew criticism for potentially undermining democratic norms.

The resistance movement encompassed multiple issue-specific campaigns and organizations. Immigration advocacy groups organized "sanctuary city" policies and legal challenges to deportation efforts. Environmental organizations coordinated opposition to Trump's climate and energy policies. Civil rights groups challenged voting restrictions and discrimination policies. Labor unions organized workplace resistance to Trump's regulatory rollbacks.

Research on the movement's effectiveness revealed mixed results. Popular resistance in Trump's first term accomplished more than many observers realize; it's just that most wins happened outside the spotlight. The most visible tactics—petitions, hashtags, occasional marches in Washington—had less impact than the quieter work of organizing in communities and workplaces.

Specific victories included limiting the effectiveness of mass deportation efforts through sanctuary policies and employer non-cooperation, constraining Trump's climate agenda through local environmental organizing and market forces, and building the political infrastructure that contributed to Democratic gains in the 2018 midterm elections.

However, the movement also faced significant limitations. Progressive movements have no direct influence over Republicans in Washington. However, they have more potential influence over businesses, lower courts, regulators and state and local politicians. The resistance movement's inability to prevent Trump's reelection in 2024 raised questions about its long-term effectiveness and strategic focus.

The movement's organizational structure reflected broader changes in American political activism. Unlike traditional social movements organized around single issues or constituencies, the Trump resistance encompassed a loose coalition of organizations with varying priorities, tactics, and ideological orientations. This diversity provided flexibility but also created coordination challenges and occasional internal conflicts.

Contemporary analysis of resistance activities during Trump's second term suggests evolution in both tactics and strategy. Protests of Trump may not look like the mass marches of 2017, but research shows they are far more numerous and frequent—while also shifting to more powerful forms of resistance. Current resistance activities include more workplace organizing, legal challenges, and non-cooperation campaigns compared to the primarily protest-focused activities of Trump's first term.

Institutional Constraints and Democratic Norms

The establishment response to Trump revealed both the strengths and limitations of American democratic institutions when confronted with a president who challenged traditional norms of governance. The conflict highlighted fundamental questions about the relationship between popular sovereignty and institutional constraints, and about how democratic systems should respond to elected leaders who reject established practices.

Traditional institutional constraints—congressional oversight, judicial review, bureaucratic expertise, and media scrutiny—proved partially effective but insufficient to fully contain Trump's exercise of presidential power. Each institution faced unique challenges in adapting to a president who did not accept the legitimacy of traditional constraints on executive authority.

Congress struggled with the limitations of its oversight powers when confronted with an administration that refused cooperation and a president whose party prioritized loyalty over institutional prerogatives. The impeachment process revealed the difficulty of holding presidents accountable when their parties control sufficient legislative votes to prevent conviction.

Federal courts provided some constraint through injunctions against controversial policies and constitutional challenges to executive overreach. However, judicial review proved slow and inconsistent, with different courts reaching different conclusions about similar policies. Trump's appointment of conservative judges also meant that the judiciary became increasingly unreliable as a check on his administration's actions.

The federal bureaucracy's resistance efforts demonstrated both the potential for career officials to constrain presidential power and the limits of such resistance in the absence of political support. Bureaucratic resistance could slow implementation of controversial policies but rarely prevented their eventual execution when the president remained committed to them.

Media scrutiny intensified during the Trump presidency, with news organizations dedicating unprecedented resources to investigating and fact-checking presidential statements and actions. However, Trump's attacks on media credibility and his cultivation of alternative information sources limited traditional journalism's ability to shape public opinion about his performance.

Lessons and Legacy of Establishment Resistance

The establishment's multifaceted response to Trump provided important insights into the resilience and vulnerabilities of American democratic institutions. The experience demonstrated that while these institutions possess significant capacity to constrain presidential power, they depend ultimately on shared commitment to democratic norms and practices that cannot be legally enforced.

The Republican Party's transformation revealed how political institutions can be captured and redirected by determined outsiders who understand how to leverage party bases against institutional elites. Trump's success in consolidating control over the GOP despite initial establishment opposition provided a template for how anti-establishment movements can achieve institutional power.

The Democratic opposition's experience illustrated both the potential and limitations of constitutional resistance. While impeachment and congressional oversight generated significant media attention and documented presidential misconduct, they proved insufficient to remove Trump from office or prevent his political comeback.

The controversy over bureaucratic resistance highlighted tensions between democratic accountability and professional expertise in federal governance. The "deep state" narrative, whether accurate or not, resonated with voters who felt that unelected officials exercised too much influence over policy outcomes.

The social movement response demonstrated the continued vitality of grassroots political organizing in American democracy. However, the movement's inability to prevent Trump's return to power raised questions about the effectiveness of protest-based politics in achieving lasting political change.

Conclusion: The Ongoing Struggle for Democratic Governance

The establishment's response to Trump represented more than opposition to a particular president or set of policies—it constituted a defense of institutional arrangements and governing norms that had structured American politics for generations. The conflict revealed deep disagreements about fundamental questions: Should popular majorities be constrained by institutional checks and professional expertise? How should democratic systems balance accountability to voters with fidelity to constitutional principles? What role should unelected officials play in policy implementation and oversight?

These questions remained unresolved as Trump returned to power in 2025, suggesting that the conflict between establishment institutions and populist politics will continue to shape American democracy. The establishment's partially successful resistance during Trump's first term provided both a model for ongoing opposition and evidence of the limitations facing institutional constraints in contemporary American politics.

The experience revealed that American democratic institutions, while resilient, are not self-sustaining. Their effectiveness depends on the willingness of political actors to respect their authority and accept their constraints. When presidents reject these norms and maintain sufficient popular support to survive institutional opposition, the balance of power in American governance shifts in ways that traditional checks and balances were not designed to address.

Understanding the establishment's response to Trump thus provides crucial insights not only into the dynamics of his presidency but into the ongoing evolution of American democracy itself. The conflict between institutional governance and populist politics that characterized the Trump era seems likely to continue influencing American political development long after Trump himself exits the political stage.

CHAPTER 12: THE 2020 ELECTION AND ITS AFTERMATH

The 2020 presidential election unfolded against a backdrop unlike any in American history. As Donald Trump sought a second term against Democratic challenger Joe Biden, the nation grappled with a global pandemic that fundamentally altered how Americans would cast their votes. What emerged was not just a contest between two visions for America's future, but a test of the democratic institutions that had guided the nation for centuries.

The election would ultimately be remembered not only for record-breaking turnout amid extraordinary circumstances, but for the unprecedented challenges that followed. From the moment polls began closing on November 3, 2020, the country witnessed events that would reshape discussions about election integrity, democratic norms, and the peaceful transfer of power. The consequences of these developments would reverberate far beyond the final vote count, leaving an indelible mark on American political discourse and the MAGA movement's understanding of electoral legitimacy.

The Pandemic Reshapes Democracy

When COVID-19 arrived in the United States in early 2020, state election boards grew concerned that the pandemic might drive voters away from the polls or that crowded polling stations would spread the virus and lead to a wave of new cases, hospitalizations, and deaths. In an effort to safely conduct the 2020 general election, many states changed their voting laws by implementing automatic voter registration, removing excuse requirements for absentee ballots, and expanding early voting windows.

The changes came in waves throughout 2020. Arkansas Governor Asa Hutchinson issued an executive order extending absentee ballot eligibility to all voters in the November 3, 2020, general election "who conclude their attendance at the polls may be a risk to their health or the health of others due to the COVID-19 pandemic." California Governor Gavin Newsom signed legislation authorizing counties to consolidate polling places, while Vermont implemented modifications to election procedures without requiring the governor's approval.

These modifications represented the most significant changes to American voting procedures in decades. States' voting procedures continued to shift as the vote neared, making it difficult for voters to keep track of what's required. What worried election experts the most was that all these challenges and changes could throw the result into doubt.

The impact was immediately visible in voting patterns. A slim majority of voters (54%) said they voted in person in November, compared with 46% who voted by absentee or mail-in ballot. About one-quarter (27%) reported having voted in person on Election Day, and an identical share said they voted in person before Election Day. This represented a dramatic shift from traditional voting patterns, with unprecedented numbers of Americans choosing alternatives to Election Day voting.

In 2020, 43% of voters cast ballots by mail and another 26% voted in person before Election Day. In 2016, 21% mailed in their ballots and 19% voted in person prior to Election Day. In the 2020 election, 69% of voters nationwide cast their ballot nontraditionally — by mail and/or before Election Day.

The demographic breakdown revealed interesting patterns. Two-thirds of Trump voters said they voted in person, compared with 42% of Biden voters. Nearly four-in-ten Trump voters (37%) said they voted in person on Election Day, while just 17% of Biden voters said they cast their ballot at a polling place on Nov. 3. This divergence would become a crucial element in post-election discussions about vote counting and election integrity.

For many voters, COVID-19 concerns directly influenced their voting method. About a quarter of Biden voters who voted in person before Election Day (27%) also pointed to COVID-19 concerns as a major reason for doing so, while just 6% of in person Trump early voters said the same. The pandemic had effectively created two different approaches to participating in democracy, largely divided along partisan lines.

Mail-In Voting: Security Measures and Controversies

The massive expansion of mail-in voting brought both new opportunities for participation and intense scrutiny of election security. Mail voting, also referred to as absentee voting, has been in use since it helped soldiers cast ballots during the Civil War. Mail voting has been increasing in usage since the 1980s, with unprecedented expansions taking place since the COVID-19 pandemic.

Election officials implemented extensive security measures to handle the surge. Every mail ballot is verified for eligibility after it is returned by the voter. Mail ballot envelopes typically require a voter's signature, identification number, or other identifying information. Before a ballot is counted, election officials check to make sure that the signature or identification number matches that which is on file. The mail ballot also must be postmarked, received by an election official, or both by a date set in state law.

The security infrastructure extended beyond basic verification. Election officials use many checks to ensure mail voting is secure against widespread fraud and tampering. The post office has multiple tracking systems to see if mail is missing and ensure voting by mail is secure. Tampering with mail ballots is a federal crime punishable with jail time.

Despite these safeguards, concerns about mail-in voting security became a significant political issue. While experts say that there is minimal risk of increased voter fraud by mail, a quarter of U.S. adults say voter fraud has been a major problem when it comes to voting by mail. Another 27% say it's been a minor problem, and an identical share say it has not been a problem at all.

The controversy was particularly intense around certain practices. Mail-in ballots also have a higher rejection rate than ballots cast in person. There is no election official in voters' home to answer questions or remedy potential problems. The U.S. Election Assistance Commission's report on the 2020 election shows that more than 500,000 of the absentee/mailed ballots returned by voters to election officials were rejected and not counted. But even more disturbing is that of the almost 91 million mailed ballots sent to voters by election officials in all states, only 70 million were returned.

Academic analysis provided a more nuanced picture. Vote by mail does introduce new risks. In theory, it could be easier for someone to fraudulently vote on behalf of someone else or for someone to tamper with the ballots in a vote-by-mail system. Furthermore, one might be more concerned about coercion or vote buying with mail ballots. In practice, however, voter fraud is very rare, and the risk of widespread fraud is probably very minimal, even with all-mail elections.

The postal service played a crucial role in the process. In the 2020 election, the post office took an average of 1.6 days to deliver a mail ballot from a voter to their election official. 97.9% of mail ballots were delivered within three days. Throughout the 2020 presidential election and amidst an uptick in mail voting, the USPS delivered 135 million ballots to and from voters — only about a third of the average volume of mail the USPS delivers in a single day.

The Legal Challenge Campaign

As vote counting continued in the days following Election Day, the Trump campaign and allied groups launched an extensive legal challenge campaign. The Trump campaign and surrogates began filing lawsuits the very same day, challenging the results on a variety of grounds well before the final votes were counted. Over the remainder of November and into December, Trump and his Republican allies filed dozens of lawsuits in key swing states that, if successful, would have given Trump the Electoral College votes needed to remain in the White House.

The scope of the litigation was unprecedented. By November 27, 2020, more than thirty of the legal challenges filed since Election Day had failed; by December 14, 2020, over fifty lawsuits had been dismissed. Among the judges who dismissed the lawsuits were some appointed by Trump himself. Judges, lawyers, and other observers described the suits as "frivolous" and "without merit."

Of the more than 60 lawsuits filed in the post-election period, Trump obtained a favorable ruling in only one case — the remainder were eventually either dismissed, settled or voluntarily withdrawn. That single victory involved a narrow procedural issue about curing mail-in ballots in Pennsylvania, which affected very few votes and was later overturned.

The legal strategy faced challenges from within. The Ohio-based Porter Wright Morris & Arthur law firm that represented the Trump campaign withdrew from the case on November 13, and Linda A. Kerns, a Republican attorney also representing the Trump campaign, asked the judge for permission to withdraw from the case on November 16. Overall, the case saw three different sets of lawyers within a week.

Court proceedings revealed the disconnect between public claims and legal arguments. When the judge asked Trump's lawyer, Rudy Giuliani, on why the plaintiffs did not advance legal claims based on voter fraud, Giuliani replied that "this is not a fraud case". Giuliani had previously made public claims of "fraud", "absolute fraud" in the election.

In multiple cases, Trump campaign lawyers explicitly acknowledged the limitations of their claims. The lawyers for the Trump campaign have signed an agreement that they "do not allege, and there is no evidence of, any fraud in connection with the challenged ballots." They also declared that they were not alleging votes from dead people, "misconduct", or "impropriety" related to those ballots, and had no evidence of such happenings.

One of the most notable rejections came from U.S. District Judge Matthew Brann in Pennsylvania. Judge Matthew W. Brann dismissed the case with prejudice on November 21, citing "strained legal arguments without merit and speculative accusations", noting that "[i]n the United States of America, this cannot justify the disenfranchisement of a single voter, let alone all the voters of its sixth most populated state." He characterized the requested remedy to disqualify nearly seven million votes as "unhinged from the underlying right being asserted."

The Supreme Court also declined to intervene significantly. The attorneys general of Georgia, Michigan, Pennsylvania, and Wisconsin asked the Supreme Court to reject the lawsuit. In their briefs, the states challenged Texas' standing, and argued that the case did not belong in the high court; that Texas has no control over how other states conduct their elections. The Court ultimately dismissed the Texas lawsuit without a hearing.

The Transition Period and Growing Tensions

The period between Election Day and Inauguration Day was marked by escalating tensions over the election results. In the months between the election and Inauguration Day (January 20), Trump engaged in multiple efforts to overturn the results. He filed numerous lawsuits, urged local and state authorities to overturn the results in their jurisdiction, pressed the Justice Department to verify unsupported claims of election fraud, and worked with congressional allies to overturn the results in Congress on January 6.

The pressure extended to state officials. On a conference call with Georgia Secretary of State Brad Raffensperger, Trump claimed that "we have won this election in Georgia," and he demanded from Raffensperger: "I just want to find, uh, 11,780 votes, which is one more than [the 11,779 vote margin of defeat] we have, because we won the state."

Meanwhile, Trump began calling for his supporters to come to Washington. Starting in December, Trump repeatedly encouraged his supporters on Twitter to show up for a "big protest" in Washington, D.C. on Jan. 6, the day that Congress accepted the Electoral College votes. At a Georgia rally Jan. 4, Trump told supporters "we're going to take what they did to us on Nov. 3. We're going to take it back."

The planning became more specific as January 6 approached. Amy Kremer of Women for America First announces a rally at the Ellipse in Washington, D.C., on January 6 starting at 7 am. An internal Capitol Police intelligence report warns that enraged protesters flanked by white supremacists and extreme militia groups are likely to arrive in Washington armed for battle and target Congress on January 6.

By January 6, Thirteen U.S. senators, including Ted Cruz and Josh Hawley, along with 100 Republican members of the House, vow to object to the election certification. The stage was set for a dramatic confrontation over the electoral process.

January 6: The Capitol Under Siege

January 6, 2021, dawned with extraordinary tension in Washington, D.C. A joint session of Congress was set to convene in the U.S. Capitol to certify Joe Biden's electoral vote win. Meanwhile, thousands of Donald Trump supporters gathered near the White House to hear him speak at noon ET.

The morning brought ominous signs. An internal Secret Service alert says that roughly 10,000 people are waiting to go through magnetometers and some are "wearing ballistic helmets, body armor and carrying radio equipment and military-grade backpacks." Somewhere between 25,000 and 30,000 people are at the Ellipse, according to a Capitol Police update that also noted rally organizers planned to march to the Capitol after Trump speech.

At his "Save America" rally, Trump delivered a lengthy speech filled with grievances about the election. His speech contained many falsehoods and misrepresentations that inflamed the crowd. Trump did not call on his supporters to use violence or enter the Capitol, but his speech was filled with violent imagery. He told supporters, "We fight like hell. And if you don't fight like hell, you're not going to have a country anymore."

However, he also said: "I know that everyone here will soon be marching over to the Capitol building to peacefully and patriotically make your voices heard."

His supporters listened. Thousands of Trump supporters, waving Trump or Confederate flags and wearing MAGA gear, descended upon the Capitol. They overwhelmed law enforcement, pushed past police barricades, and temporarily stopped Congress from counting electoral votes.

The situation deteriorated rapidly. Within 36 hours, five people died: one was shot by the Capitol Police, another died of a drug overdose, and three died of natural causes, including a police officer who died of a stroke a day after being assaulted by rioters and collapsing at the Capitol.

Inside the Capitol, the scene was chaotic. Secret Service agents whisk Pence off the Senate floor. A few minutes later, Pelosi is ushered off the House floor. The Senate is called to recess, and the House is called to recess shortly after. The building goes into lockdown.

While lawmakers and staff were shepherded to secure locations or barricaded behind doors, the rioters pushed past severely outnumbered Capitol Police officers, breaking windows and vandalizing offices, many with disturbingly violent intentions toward members of Congress and Vice President Mike Pence for their having refused to succumb to Trump's attempts to overturn the election in his favor.

The violence was significant. According to a Justice Department report released in July 2021, approximately 140 Capitol and Metropolitan police officers were criminally assaulted by the rioters in the January 6 attack. The rioters caused an estimated $1.5 million in damage to the Capitol building.

Trump's response during the crisis became a subject of intense scrutiny. Public reporting has revealed that, during the attack's first three hours, Trump watched the violence play out on TV, ignoring calls from allies and others to call off the mob. Trump tweets: "Mike Pence didn't have the courage to do what should have been done to protect our Country and our Constitution."

Eventually, Congress reconvened to complete its constitutional duty. After more than four hours, the mob was cleared and Trump's Twitter and Facebook accounts were temporarily locked for policy violations. Congress reconvened to certify the electoral-vote tally. Around 3:40 a.m., more than 13 hours after the Capitol was breached, Vice President Pence officially affirmed the election results, declaring Biden the winner.

The Investigations and Aftermath

The events of January 6 triggered multiple investigations and accountability efforts. On January 13, 2021, the House of Representatives, by a vote of 232 to 197, adopted a single article of impeachment against Trump for incitement of insurrection. This made Trump the first president to be impeached twice, though he was subsequently acquitted by the Senate.

Law enforcement conducted extensive investigations. AP Reporters went looking for cases of voter fraud in six states that Trump has challenged, and they found fewer than 475 potential instances out of more than 25 million votes cast, a number that would not have come close to changing the outcome.

There are numerous procedures, protocols in place, guardrails to ensure that every ballot is accounted for. Mail ballots that are sent out, they are logged. Every mail ballot that is returned is logged. They go through various security checks in a number of states. They do — they conduct signature verification.

The judicial system's response was consistent across jurisdictions. Despite their different backgrounds, judges came to the same conclusions and rejected the Trump campaign's allegations. Across more than 60 cases in 12 states, judges found that the challenges to the election outcome came up short.

The Enduring Impact

The 2020 election and its aftermath fundamentally altered American political discourse. The events demonstrated both the resilience of democratic institutions and their vulnerability to unprecedented challenges. The resoluteness of the judiciary in this time of turmoil provided inspiration and calm to the country. While the guardrails of democracy generally may need our attention and shoring up, the judiciary rose to the occasion without missing a step.

The election introduced new realities about voting in America. Expanded voting options enhance election integrity by spreading voting out over several days rather than concentrating it on a single day. The success of early in-person and mail voting was on full display during the 2020 general election. Amid an ongoing global pandemic and record turnout, more than 69% of voters nationwide cast their ballot before Election Day—up from about 40% of voters just four years earlier.

For the MAGA movement, the 2020 election became a defining moment that shaped its understanding of electoral legitimacy and institutional trust. The questions raised about election integrity, while largely rejected by courts and election officials, resonated deeply with Trump supporters who viewed the outcome as fundamentally flawed.

Ongoing scrutiny, audits, and analysis by actors across the political spectrum have repeatedly upheld the 2020 general election as the most secure in American history. Yet the political impact of the challenges extended far beyond the courtroom, influencing subsequent elections, voting laws, and the broader conversation about democratic participation in America.

The legacy of the 2020 election continues to shape American politics, demonstrating how a global pandemic, changing voting procedures, legal challenges, and unprecedented post-election events can combine to test the foundations of democratic governance. The ultimate certification of the results affirmed the continuity of American democratic traditions, but the process revealed new vulnerabilities and challenges that would influence electoral discourse for years to come.

CHAPTER 13: ELECTION INTEGRITY AND DEMOCRATIC NORMS

In the aftermath of the 2020 election, America found itself grappling with fundamental questions about the very foundation of its democracy. The concept of election integrity—once a largely technical concern discussed primarily among election officials and policy experts—suddenly became a defining political battleground that would reshape how Americans think about voting, governance, and democratic legitimacy itself.

The debates that emerged were not merely academic discussions about electoral processes, but visceral conflicts that touched the core of American identity. For millions of Americans, particularly those within the MAGA movement, concerns about election integrity represented existential threats to democratic self-governance. For others, these same concerns appeared to be unfounded challenges that themselves threatened democratic stability. This fundamental disagreement about the nature and extent of electoral problems would prove to have far-reaching consequences that extended well beyond any single election cycle, fundamentally altering the relationship between citizens and their democratic institutions.

The Statistical Reality of Voter Fraud

At the heart of many post-2020 election debates lay claims about widespread voter fraud. Understanding the actual prevalence of fraud requires examining the statistical evidence that has emerged from extensive investigations and research conducted by organizations across the political spectrum.

The Heritage Foundation, a conservative think tank famous for its comprehensive tracking of election fraud cases, maintains the most detailed database of proven voter fraud instances in the United States. To come up with thousands of instances of voter fraud around the country, Heritage staff had to go back decades in time where there have been hundreds of millions of votes cast and a very small number of cases of election fraud have been found, none of which affected election outcomes.

The statistical picture that emerges from this data is striking. In Arizona, Heritage had to go back 25 years, over which there were 36 elections held and 42,626,379 ballots cast, in order to come up with 36 cases of fraud. The percentage of fraudulent votes was a minuscule .0000845%, and no election outcome was altered by ballot fraud throughout that time period. Similarly, in the highly contested state of Pennsylvania, Heritage data goes back 30 years and covers 32 elections with over 100 million votes cast and found only 39 cases of voter fraud.

Even more targeted investigations of specific elections have yielded similarly low fraud rates. In December 2021, the Associated Press released a detailed fact-check which found fewer than 475 instances of voter fraud out of an estimated 25 million votes cast in the six battleground states in 2020. These cases involved both Democrats and Republicans and were almost always caught before the votes were counted.

Recent investigations by Republican-led states have reinforced these findings. In Ohio, Republican Secretary of State Frank LaRose announced in 2022 his office had found 75 voters who allegedly cast a ballot in the state and another state in 2020. Almost 6 million ballots were cast in Ohio that year. Even with increased enforcement efforts, LaRose's office said they had referred a total of 630 cases to prosecutors "over the course of multiple elections" — while also noting "voter fraud continues to be exceedingly rare" in the state.

The nature of many fraud cases also reveals important nuances. A lot of these cases involve people who at one point lost their voting rights due to a felony conviction, and many instances involved ineligible voters who voted "accidentally in good faith, believing that they were eligible" rather than intentional fraud designed to manipulate election outcomes.

Academic analysis has further reinforced these findings. We see nothing in these statistical tests that supports Trump's claim of a stolen election, concluded researchers from Stanford and other universities who conducted comprehensive statistical analysis of 2020 election claims. The study found that the 2020 election was remarkable in many ways (e.g., unusually high levels of mail-in voting and turnout), and election administration may well have been imperfect. But we see nothing in these statistical tests that supports Trump's claim of a stolen election.

Multiple safeguards help explain these low fraud rates. States have very effective protections in place to prevent and detect voter fraud, including routine removal of ineligible or deceased voters from rolls and tools like the Electronic Registration Information Center (ERIC) that help states share voter data. These protections work at multiple levels, from initial voter registration through ballot counting and certification.

The Great Divergence: State Election Law Changes Since 2020

The 2020 election triggered an unprecedented wave of legislative activity across the country, as states grappled with lessons learned from conducting elections during a pandemic and responding to various concerns about election security and access. However, rather than moving in a unified direction, states have pursued dramatically different approaches, creating what experts describe as a widening divide in American election administration.

In nine battleground states in this year's presidential elections, voting rules will look considerably different than they did four years ago. In the years since the 2020 election, many states have aggressively attempted to restrict voting access. Limiting absentee voting has been the most prevalent tactic. At the same time, other states have moved in the opposite direction, expanding voting access and opportunities.

The numbers tell a story of dramatic legislative activity. In 2024, at least 10 states enacted 19 restrictive laws. Overall, at least 317 restrictive bills were considered in 40 states. Since the 2020 presidential election, at least 30 states enacted 79 restrictive laws. However, these restrictive measures were more than offset by expansive legislation. In 2024, at least 21 states enacted 32 expansive laws. Overall, at least 648 expansive voting bills were considered in 44 states and Washington, DC. At least 42 states plus Washington, DC, have enacted 172 expansive laws since January 2021.

Georgia became a focal point of post-2020 legislative changes. In early 2021, the Georgia legislature passed Senate Bill 202. This 98-page law takes aim at all sorts of ways people vote. On mail voting, it cuts the window to request a ballot by more than half, requires counties to wait longer to mail out ballots, establishes new ID rules, bars officials from mailing ballots that voters have not requested, and severely restricts the availability of drop box locations and hours (especially in large cities).

Other states pursued different approaches. Forty-seven new state laws expanding access to voting were enacted in 23 states — 13 of which are controlled by Democrats and four which have split control. That's more than twice the number of "expansion" laws as last year. A quarter of these new laws — six each — came from Michigan and New York.

The legislative changes have created a complex patchwork of voting requirements. Since the last presidential election, at least 29 states have enacted dozens of laws that, among other things, make voter ID rules stricter, reduce opportunities to vote by mail, and make ballot collection and voter assistance more difficult. These changes affect different aspects of the voting process: This November, voters in at least nine states face stringent new voter ID requirements that were not in place for the 2020 election, while at least 19 states have new mail voting restrictions in place for the first time in a presidential election.

The pattern of change has been largely partisan. Republican-led states like Arizona passing new restrictive voting laws, while Democratic states such as Illinois have increased voters' ballot access. However, some states have enacted mixed approaches. Texas, for instance, passed legislation allowing fewer polling places in some locations and sharply increasing state power over elections in Democratic Harris County. But it also enacted laws mandating expanded in-person early voting access, adding the option to rectify early voting application mistakes and providing further accommodations for people with disabilities.

An entirely new category of legislation has also emerged. Since 2022, the Brennan Center has been tracking another category of legislation that subverts democracy: election interference legislation. These measures allow for partisan interference in elections or threaten the people and processes that make elections work. So far this year, at least 2 states — South Dakota and Louisiana — have each enacted an election interference law. Overall, at least 60 election interference bills have been considered in 21 states.

Political scientists have noted that these changes reflect broader philosophical differences about election administration. It really varies by state whether the norm is mail-in voting or Election Day voting or early in-person voting, and it's constantly changing, so it's hard to keep up. The result has been a widening fault line between states expanding voting access and those restricting it.

Social Media: The New Battleground for Electoral Information

The role of social media in shaping public understanding of elections has undergone dramatic changes since 2020, with platforms adopting increasingly different approaches to content moderation and election-related information. These changes have significant implications for how Americans receive and process information about electoral processes.

In the run-up to and aftermath of the 2020 election, major social media platforms implemented extensive measures to combat misinformation. However, the landscape has shifted considerably since then. Studies have shown that YouTube has backed off enforcing prior commitments to crack down on videos pushing the big lie, the false idea that the 2020 election was stolen. And many YouTube, TikTok and X provocateurs are going viral by seeding doubt about the 2024 result already.

The transformation has been particularly dramatic on X (formerly Twitter). The most obvious change is Twitter, now X. Elon Musk has transformed the platform into a megaphone for the reelection of Donald Trump. And with that has come droves of MAGA fans and very few content rules that would otherwise have taken down false claims about the election. This shift has had broader implications across the social media ecosystem, as researchers say X has become something of a free-for-all with, you know, very few consequences from Washington. And that has given other social media sites permission to just be looser with their rules.

Research shows that nearly all of the social media platforms are, quote, "backsliding on commitments they made in the wake of the 2020 election". This represents a significant change from the approach taken during the 2020 election cycle, when platforms were more actively monitoring and moderating election-related content.

The effects of social media on political knowledge and behavior are complex and nuanced. Large-scale experimental research conducted during the 2020 election found that Facebook deactivation reduced an index of political participation (driven mainly by reduced participation online), while also finding that Facebook deactivation had no significant effect on an index of knowledge, but secondary analyses suggest that it reduced knowledge of general news while possibly also decreasing belief in misinformation circulating online.

The spread of election-related misinformation on social media follows predictable patterns. Social media allows for the rapid spread of disinformation. If we can't even agree on fairly straightforward things, and truth becomes entirely subjective to your identity affiliation, it can be super harmful to democracy overall. Research has shown that disinformation remained a major player that even grew by factor four between the 2016 and 2020 elections.

The role of social media in political campaigns has also evolved significantly. Political campaigns have been repurposed to accommodate the importance of social media platforms as powerful tools for communication, outreach, and influence. The 2024 U.S. presidential election highlighted the key role of social media presence in reaching the American audience. Campaigns now leverage viral campaigning—using reposts, retweets, and the generation of new visual content—a single message can go viral and reach millions instantly.

However, the effectiveness of social media in actually changing political behavior remains limited. Studies suggest that AI's effectiveness in swaying voters appears limited. Such conclusions have been drawn in the context of other elections. Instead, social media appears to be more effective at reinforcing existing beliefs and amplifying exposure to like-minded opinions leads to limited exposure to diverse perspectives and contributes to political polarization.

Public opinion research reveals growing concern about election misinformation on social media platforms. Americans express growing concern about election-related misinformation on social media, with 65% believing the problem has worsened since 2020. There is broad, bipartisan support for social media companies taking a more active role in content moderation, with 71% of respondents favoring platforms prioritizing the prevention of false claims over unrestricted expression.

Foreign interference through social media remains a persistent concern. When foreign governments or agents of foreign governments intentionally try to undermine U.S. election outcomes, they tend to spread false or inflated claims across social media to purposefully undermine public confidence in election processes and election results. Intelligence assessments have documented how Russian efforts attempted to influence voters via misinformation and unsubstantiated allegations against Biden. These allegations were repeated by the media and shared across social media platforms.

The challenge of distinguishing reliable from unreliable information has become increasingly difficult for ordinary users. Studies indicate that social media can spread false claims rapidly and increase selective exposure to attitude-consistent news and information. These tendencies may be exacerbated by design and platform features such as algorithmic feeds and community structures. Research shows that Facebook played a central role in spreading content from untrustworthy websites relative to other platforms.

The Erosion and Evolution of Democratic Trust

Perhaps the most significant long-term consequence of the post-2020 election debates has been their impact on public trust in democratic institutions. This erosion of confidence represents a fundamental challenge to the stability and legitimacy of American democracy, with effects that extend far beyond any single election cycle.

The decline in electoral trust has been measurable and concerning. An ABC NEWS/Washington Post survey found that only 20% feel "very confident" in the integrity of the U.S. election system. Furthermore, 56% of respondents of a recent CNN poll said that they have "little or no confidence" that the elections represent the will of the people. This skepticism extends to younger Americans, as 42% of the Harvard Youth Poll participants believe that their vote does not make a difference.

The partisan nature of this trust erosion is particularly striking. Recent polls show public trust in the integrity of U.S. elections is decreasing, largely among Republicans. However, experts emphasize that this doesn't signal that our elections are getting less reliable, UC Berkeley scholars said. In fact, elections in the U.S. are more secure and the results are more accurate than 20 years ago.

The disconnect between actual election security and public perception represents a significant challenge for democratic governance. Through a technical lens, U.S. elections are very secure. In the early 2000s, the technical risks of voting equipment getting hacked was high. Now, many risks have been partly or wholly resolved. Technical experts note that voting machines must meet protective specifications, and a subset of the votes are audited manually in many states to ensure these systems tallied them accurately.

The most significant threats to electoral integrity may not be technical at all. Today, I think the biggest risk is the human element — disinformation, propaganda, the manipulation through the media, targeted efforts to try to get particular populations to vote or not vote and attempts by other countries to breed chaos or interfere in our election, noted one expert.

Despite declining trust in specific aspects of elections, comparative institutional trust reveals a more complex picture. The public ranks election administration well in terms of trust when compared to other institutions—outranking Congress, the Executive Branch, and the Press. In 2016, 95 percent of people gave a good or excellent job performance ratings for their poll workers and nearly 60 percent gave high rankings to their local election officials.

The implications of decreased electoral trust extend beyond voting itself. The implications of this trend are huge, as decreased confidence in the system decreases civic engagement. For instance, in a survey by Howard University's Digital Informers, respondents were asked, "do you believe that your vote really counts?"; 26% of respondents believed that their vote did not count.

Broader patterns of institutional trust provide important context. When the National Election Study began asking about trust in government in 1958, about three-quarters of Americans trusted the federal government to do the right thing almost always or most of the time. Trust in government began eroding during the 1960s, amid the escalation of the Vietnam War, and the decline continued in the 1970s with the Watergate scandal and worsening economic struggles. The current period represents a continuation of longer-term trends, with since 2007, the shares saying they can trust the government always or most of the time have not been higher than 30%.

The global context reveals that challenges to electoral trust are not unique to the United States. Public trust in elections is being targeted around the world by a series of disinformation campaigns from a range of international players. This is giving rise to an increasing lack of trust in electoral systems. The concern is that if disinformation creates a widespread public belief that elections are "stolen" or manipulated, it undermines belief in public institutions that are essential to democratic governance.

The challenge of rebuilding trust requires multifaceted approaches. One of the most dangerous consequences of the concerted disinformation efforts intended to undermine public confidence in our democratic institutions has been the attacks on the fairness of our elections. Experts emphasize that it is imperative that all media outlets focus their efforts on rebutting mistruths and rehabilitating the public's confidence in our elections.

Understanding why misinformation spreads is crucial to addressing trust deficits. The power of misinformation lies not in its factual content, but in the emotional response it elicits. Research shows that the most likely predictor for whether someone will trust an image is whether their own views align with that image, highlighting the role of confirmation bias in shaping perceptions of electoral information.

The Path Forward: Balancing Security and Democracy

The debates over election integrity and democratic norms that have emerged since 2020 reflect fundamental tensions in American democracy. On one side are legitimate concerns about maintaining the highest possible standards for electoral security and public confidence. On the other side are equally legitimate concerns about preserving access to the fundamental right to vote and maintaining faith in democratic institutions.

The statistical evidence clearly shows that large-scale voter fraud capable of changing election outcomes is extremely rare in American elections. At the same time, the perception of fraud problems has had real consequences for public trust and civic engagement. Similarly, while states have pursued different approaches to election law changes, these modifications reflect genuine policy differences about how to balance security, access, and administrative efficiency.

Social media's evolving role in electoral discourse presents both opportunities and challenges. While these platforms can facilitate political engagement and information sharing, they also create new vectors for the rapid spread of both accurate information and misinformation. The retreat from content moderation policies implemented during 2020 suggests that the relationship between social media companies and election integrity will continue to evolve.

Perhaps most concerning is the erosion of trust in democratic institutions, which threatens the foundation of democratic governance itself. While some decline in institutional trust reflects broader historical patterns, the specific targeting of electoral legitimacy represents a unique challenge to democratic stability.

The path forward requires acknowledging both the reality of electoral security—that American elections are highly secure and fraud is rare—while also addressing the genuine concerns that drive public skepticism. This includes continued investment in election security measures, transparent communication about electoral processes, media literacy education, and sustained efforts to combat deliberate disinformation campaigns.

Ultimately, the health of American democracy depends not just on the technical integrity of elections, but on public confidence in that integrity. Rebuilding and maintaining that confidence requires ongoing work from election officials, political leaders, media organizations, civic groups, and citizens themselves. The stakes of this work extend far beyond any single election, touching the very foundations of democratic governance and the peaceful transfer of power that has characterized American democracy for more than two centuries.

The MAGA movement's focus on election integrity, regardless of one's perspective on specific claims, has undeniably elevated public attention to electoral processes in ways that may ultimately strengthen democracy through increased civic engagement and oversight. The challenge lies in channeling this heightened attention toward constructive improvements rather than destructive mistrust. The future of American democracy may well depend on successfully meeting this challenge.

CHAPTER 14: THE MOVEMENT BEYOND TRUMP

As Donald Trump's second presidential term progresses, a fascinating transformation is unfolding within American conservatism. What began as a movement built around one man's distinctive political brand has evolved into something far more complex and enduring—a generational shift that extends well beyond Trump himself. The MAGA movement has successfully created institutional structures, developed emerging leaders, and captured the imagination of America's youngest voters in ways that suggest its influence will persist long after Trump exits the political stage.

The most striking aspect of this evolution is how thoroughly the movement has embedded itself within the Republican Party's infrastructure and political culture. Rather than remaining a purely Trump-centric phenomenon, MAGA has become the dominant strain of American conservatism, reshaping everything from local school board elections to the highest levels of federal government. This transformation represents not just a political shift, but a fundamental reimagining of what it means to be conservative in 21st-century America—one that prioritizes populist appeals, cultural battles, and institutional skepticism over traditional conservative orthodoxies.

The New Generation of Republican Leaders

The question of who might succeed Trump has become one of the most closely watched aspects of contemporary Republican politics. Unlike previous transitions where establishment figures typically dominated succession discussions, the MAGA movement has produced a distinctive cohort of leaders who combine Trump's populist appeal with their own unique political brands.

Vice President JD Vance stands as the most obvious inheritor of Trump's mantle. The vice president has long ago abandoned the criticisms of Trump that he once leveled. Despite the vigor of those critiques — he mulled to a friend in 2016 whether Trump could end up being "America's Hitler" — he appears to have been forgiven by the MAGA base. Vance's transformation from Never Trumper to Trump's chosen successor represents perhaps the most dramatic political evolution in modern American politics.

With Trump's blessing, Vance is finance chair for the Republican National Committee — a position that will keep him connected to some of the party's top donors between now and 2028. His unique background as the author of "Hillbilly Elegy" gives him credibility with the working-class voters who form the core of Trump's coalition, while his Ivy League education and venture capital experience provide establishment credentials that Trump himself lacked.

Early polling reflects Vance's frontrunner status. The survey, conducted by Morning Consult between December 6 and 8, 2024, among 994 registered voters, shows Vance and Trump Jr. each securing 30%

support among likely Republican voters. However, the political landscape remains fluid, and Vance's success will ultimately depend on his ability to maintain Trump's coalition while expanding its appeal.

Florida Governor Ron DeSantis represents a different model of post-Trump Republican leadership. Despite his bruising 2024 primary loss to Trump, DeSantis always remained rather popular — almost as popular as Trump; he just wasn't Trump. His governance of Florida during the COVID-19 pandemic established him as a national conservative figure, and his legislative achievements on issues ranging from education to immigration have provided a template for MAGA governance at the state level.

DeSantis's approach differs from Trump's in significant ways. Where Trump relies heavily on personality and media spectacle, DeSantis has focused on policy implementation and institutional change. DeSantis really saw his national profile skyrocket during the coronavirus pandemic, when he encouraged Florida officials to take a more hands-off approach to restrictions and became a vocal opponent of Anthony Fauci. This positioning allowed him to capture Trump-style resistance to elite opinion while maintaining the demeanor of a serious policy maker.

Vivek Ramaswamy represents yet another model—the entrepreneur-politician who brings private sector experience to conservative governance. Entrepreneur Vivek Ramaswamy has been rapidly building his political profile since his 2024 Republican presidential primary run. However, unlike Rubio and DeSantis, Ramaswamy avoided attacking Trump. His decision to run for Ohio governor in 2026 reflects a strategic approach to building the governing credentials necessary for a future presidential run.

The emergence of these figures reflects a broader pattern within the Republican Party. Unlike the establishment-dominated succession processes of previous eras, the post-Trump GOP has elevated leaders who explicitly embrace populist themes and cultural conservatism. This represents a fundamental shift in the party's intellectual and political center of gravity.

Secretary of State Marco Rubio's evolution exemplifies this transformation. Once a vocal Trump critic during the 2016 primary, Rubio has reinvented himself as a champion of Trump-style foreign policy and economic nationalism. Trump seemed to put Vance and Rubio on an equal 2028 plane in the "Meet the Press" interview, suggesting that Trump sees multiple potential successors rather than a single chosen heir.

The diversity of potential successors—from Vance's working-class populism to DeSantis's policy-focused governance to Ramaswamy's entrepreneurial background—suggests that the post-Trump Republican Party will likely maintain MAGA's core themes while allowing for different stylistic and tactical approaches.

State-Level Conservative Victories

While national political attention focuses on presidential contests, some of the most significant long-term impacts of the MAGA movement have occurred at the state level. Republican governors and state legislatures have implemented sweeping conservative policy agendas that provide both a governing template and a political foundation for future national campaigns.

The scope of Republican control at the state level is striking. Currently, there are 27 Republican governors and 23 Democratic governors. This represents not just electoral success, but governing opportunity on an unprecedented scale. Republican governors have used their positions to implement policies that would have been politically impossible at the federal level, creating laboratories for conservative governance.

Florida under Ron DeSantis has emerged as the premier example of MAGA-style state governance. The party now holds veto-proof majorities in Florida and Ohio. In these states, many conservative policy priorities have already been enacted or proposed, such as permitless gun carrying and restrictions on teaching about gender or sexuality in schools. DeSantis's approach has combined traditional conservative policies with newer culture war issues, creating a comprehensive conservative governing agenda.

Texas under Greg Abbott has similarly pushed the boundaries of conservative governance, particularly on immigration and border security. Abbott is seen as a staunch Trump ally, particularly on the key issue of immigration and securing the southern border. Like DeSantis in Florida, Abbott has sought to boost his state's working relationship with the Trump administration on immigration. Abbott's willingness to challenge federal authority on immigration enforcement has established Texas as a model for conservative resistance to federal overreach.

The coordination between state-level Republicans and the Trump administration has accelerated during Trump's second term. Republican lawmakers and governors in a handful of states, including Idaho, New Hampshire, Georgia, Texas, Kansas and Oklahoma have created DOGE task forces or new state legislature committees. This represents an unprecedented level of coordination between federal and state conservative governance.

Iowa Governor Kim Reynolds exemplifies this collaborative approach. Iowa Republican Gov. Kim Reynolds, who signed an executive order last week launching a DOGE task force in her state, has described the effort of an extension of the work Iowa began a few years ago. Iowa's "alignment" process saved the state $217 million in 18 months, Reynolds said. This demonstrates how state-level innovations can influence and complement federal policy initiatives.

The state-level success of Republican governors has also provided a pipeline for national political talent. Several GOP governors are in prime position to challenge Vance and any other lawmaker during the presidential primary. Gov. Ron DeSantis (R-FL) seemed left for dead after losing the primary to Trump in January, but after patching up their relationship, the Florida governor could likely decide to run for president.

Beyond individual governors, the broader pattern of Republican state-level success has created institutional advantages that extend beyond any single election cycle. Republican governors brushed off challengers, even in races that were thought to be close. In Georgia, Gov. Brian Kemp defeated Democrat Stacy Abrams for the second time, and by a wider margin. This demonstrates the durability of conservative governance at the state level.

The policy innovations emerging from Republican-controlled states provide a template for future national conservative governance. From education reform to regulatory reduction to immigration enforcement, state-level Republican leaders have demonstrated that conservative policies can be implemented effectively and maintain public support.

Institutional Transformation and Lasting Changes

Perhaps the most significant long-term impact of the Trump/MAGA movement has been its systematic transformation of American governmental institutions. These changes extend far beyond personnel decisions or policy preferences, representing fundamental alterations to how the federal government operates and understands its own role.

The transformation has been particularly pronounced in regulatory agencies and federal bureaucracy. Former President Trump comes along and passes one of the largest tax reforms, deepest tax cuts in American history. All the experts agree on that. So, a lot of what he did happened quickly. This rapid pace of change has characterized Trump's approach to institutional reform throughout his presidency.

The second Trump administration has accelerated these institutional changes. During its first few weeks, the Trump Administration has unleashed a flurry of measures to radically reshape the federal government. Many of these moves are overtly unlawful. However, the administration's approach reflects a broader philosophy about the proper scope and role of federal institutions.

One of the most significant areas of change has been in the relationship between the president and independent agencies. The Administration has announced that it believes that restrictions on the President's power to remove members of independent agencies are unconstitutional, notwithstanding the

Supreme Court's unanimous decision approving such conditions. This represents a fundamental challenge to the post-New Deal administrative state.

The judicial branch has also experienced significant transformation, though in more subtle ways. Trump's campaign to convince governors to take actions to suppress the vote remains a huge problem for democracy but it is succeeding not because Trump had dictatorial powers over the states but because he has like-minded allies in many state houses and state legislatures. The appointment of conservative judges at all levels has created lasting institutional change that will persist well beyond Trump's presidency.

Federal agencies have undergone systematic restructuring and reorientation. The regulatory tracker was last updated on June 25, 2025. Rules are up to date as of June 17, 2025. As the Trump administration returns to office for a second term with renewed deregulatory ambitions, the executive branch and its agencies are implementing significant policy changes. These changes represent not just policy adjustments, but fundamental alterations to how agencies understand their missions and responsibilities.

The Department of Education has been a particular focus of institutional reform efforts. The Trump administration has acted illegally and unconstitutionally in ways that weaken our democratic institutions, slow down our economy, roll back protections for public health and the environment, and put health care and Social Security benefits at risk for millions of Americans. Critics argue that these changes represent dangerous overreach, while supporters see them as necessary corrections to decades of bureaucratic expansion.

The lasting impact of these institutional changes cannot be overstated. Trump was really lucky, because he came to power as a result of the accumulation of tipping points, or windows of opportunity. And once in power, he also experienced windows of opportunity of various sorts. The systematic nature of these changes suggests that they will persist even after Trump leaves office, creating a different kind of federal government than existed before 2017.

The Rising Generation of Conservative Activists

Perhaps the most surprising and potentially significant development within the MAGA movement has been its success in attracting young Americans, particularly men, to conservative politics. This represents a dramatic shift from historical patterns where younger voters typically lean left, potentially reshaping the future of American politics.

The data revealing this generational shift is striking. According to the latest Yale Youth Poll, there is an 18-point gap between younger and older members of Generation Z. Those between the ages of 22-29 favor

Democrats by 6.4 points, while those aged 18-21 favor Republicans by 11.7 points. This suggests that the youngest American voters are significantly more conservative than their slightly older peers.

The COVID-19 pandemic appears to have played a crucial role in this political realignment. Youth political analyst Rachel Janfaza broke Gen Z down into two groups, with one being comprised of those who graduated before the COVID-19 pandemic and those who were in high school or middle school during this time. The latter group appears to view policies that fall under "MAGA" as counter-cultural and more appealing.

This generational divide has been particularly pronounced among young men. Young Gen Z white men—mainly those without college degrees—voted overwhelmingly for Trump (67 percent), which is eerily similar to their just-older millennial peers (also 67 percent). The appeal of Trump's brand of masculinity and his explicit appeals to young men appear to have resonated with this demographic in unprecedented ways.

Organizations like Turning Point USA have played a crucial role in mobilizing young conservatives. Since 2015, Trump's MAGA movement has broken the "three pillars of neoliberalism," Kirk said in an interview with the Deseret News: "invade the world, invite the world and import a bunch of stuff you don't need from China". Charlie Kirk's organization has created institutional infrastructure for young conservative activism that didn't exist in previous generations.

The cultural dimension of this conservative youth movement is particularly significant. This month, Turning Point USA's Young Women's Leadership Summit brought together thousands of conservative women in their teens and twenties. A common theme among speakers and attendees was that women should forego higher education and focus on becoming homemakers and mothers. This represents a direct challenge to mainstream feminist messaging and suggests a broader cultural counter-revolution among young Americans.

Even at traditionally liberal institutions like Harvard, conservative activism is experiencing unprecedented growth. When Koerner was a freshman, he says, the club might have drawn 20 to 30 people to an event featuring a conservative speaker. Now, such events can attract over 100 students. This expansion of conservative influence at elite educational institutions suggests that the movement's appeal extends beyond its traditional working-class base.

The role of social media in this generational shift cannot be underestimated. The percentage of young voters getting their news from TikTok more than quadrupled over the past four years, Shor found, increasing from 9% to 39%, with those relying on the platform for news shifting 6-points toward Trump.

The democratization of media through social platforms has allowed conservative voices to reach young audiences in ways that traditional media could not.

The psychological appeal of conservative politics to young men appears particularly strong. Why do they vote? Why are they drawn to conservative politics? Because they feel the voices in conservative politics don't put them on the bottom of the hierarchy. This suggests that the conservative movement's success with young men reflects deeper cultural and psychological dynamics rather than merely partisan political appeals.

The implications of this generational shift extend far beyond immediate electoral considerations. Young voters are expected to dominate the electorate over the next decade. In 2024 alone, close to 40% of millennials and Gen Zers are expected to vote. If current trends continue, the Republican Party could find itself with a significant generational advantage that would fundamentally alter American political competition.

The Institutional Foundation for Long-Term Success

The transformation of American conservatism under Trump's influence represents more than just electoral success or policy changes—it reflects the creation of a comprehensive institutional infrastructure designed to sustain and expand conservative influence across multiple generations and political cycles.

This infrastructure spans from grassroots organizations like Turning Point USA to state-level policy institutes to federal agencies reshaped by conservative appointees. The result is a movement that has embedded itself deeply within American political institutions and culture, creating multiple pathways for continued influence even as individual leaders come and go.

The success of Republican governors in implementing comprehensive conservative policy agendas has provided both governing models and political talent pipelines for future national campaigns. These state-level laboratories have demonstrated that conservative policies can be implemented effectively and maintain public support, providing templates for future federal governance.

The capture of younger voters, particularly young men, represents perhaps the most significant long-term asset for the conservative movement. Unlike previous generations of conservative activists who often moved left as they aged, the current cohort of young conservatives appears to be maintaining their political orientation as they mature. This suggests that the MAGA movement's influence will persist and potentially expand as these young activists assume leadership roles.

The systematic transformation of federal institutions, while controversial and legally contested, has created lasting changes to how the American government operates. These changes have been designed to persist beyond any single administration, creating structural advantages for future conservative governance.

The combination of institutional change, generational appeal, state-level success, and emerging leadership suggests that the MAGA movement has successfully evolved beyond its origins as a Trump-centered phenomenon. While Trump's personal influence remains crucial, the movement has created independent sources of political power and cultural influence that will likely outlast his direct political involvement.

The ultimate test of this transformation will come in the 2028 election and beyond, when the movement must demonstrate its ability to maintain power and influence without Trump at its center. Early indicators suggest that this transition may be more successful than many observers initially expected, but the final verdict will depend on the next generation of conservative leaders' ability to maintain the coalition while adapting to new political and cultural challenges.

The MAGA movement's evolution beyond Trump represents one of the most significant political transformations in modern American history—one whose ultimate implications are still unfolding but whose influence seems likely to shape American politics for decades to come.

CHAPTER 15: LESSONS AND THE FUTURE OF AMERICAN GREATNESS

The story of America's encounter with the MAGA movement is far from over, but enough time has passed to begin drawing meaningful lessons from this extraordinary chapter in the nation's political evolution. What began as a slogan on a red hat has become something much larger—a lens through which to examine the deepest tensions and aspirations of American society. The movement's impact extends far beyond electoral politics, revealing fundamental questions about who Americans are as a people, what institutions can and cannot withstand, and how the United States will position itself in an increasingly complex global landscape.

The MAGA phenomenon represents more than a political campaign or policy agenda; it functions as what scholars call "a status-based social movement" organized around "a shared perception of lost honor, declining esteem, and institutional disrespect." This characterization helps explain both the movement's remarkable staying power and its polarizing effect on American society. Understanding these dynamics—and their implications for the future—requires an honest assessment of what this political moment has taught us about ourselves and our democratic institutions.

What the Movement Reveals About American Society

Perhaps the most striking revelation from the MAGA era has been the depth of social and cultural divisions that many Americans thought had been largely resolved or were steadily improving. When asked what "Make America Great Again" means to them, Americans provide dramatically different answers that reveal fundamentally incompatible worldviews about the country's past, present, and future. These divergent interpretations expose fault lines that run much deeper than traditional partisan disagreements over policy.

Throughout Trump's presidency, the nation witnessed "extraordinary fissures in American society" that went beyond normal political disagreements. The movement has laid bare what sociologists call "sequential polarization"—the way geographic, economic, and cultural divisions have reinforced each other over decades. Rural and small-town Americans increasingly see themselves as forgotten by a system that prioritizes urban coastal elites, while urban Americans view rural concerns as rooted in outdated thinking that resists necessary social progress.

The movement has also revealed the extent to which Americans have come to inhabit separate information ecosystems, with "around three-quarters of Americans saying most Republican and Democratic voters disagreed not just over political plans and policies, but over 'basic facts.'" This breakdown in shared epistemological foundations represents something qualitatively different from previous periods of political tension. When citizens cannot agree on fundamental questions of what constitutes reliable information or legitimate authority, democratic deliberation becomes nearly impossible.

Economic anxiety, while real, proved insufficient to explain the movement's appeal. Many MAGA supporters experienced improving economic conditions during periods when their political activation intensified, suggesting that the movement taps into something deeper than material concerns. Research shows it addresses "lost honor, declining esteem, and institutional disrespect"—fundamentally cultural and psychological needs that conventional politics struggles to address.

The movement has also demonstrated how quickly and dramatically public attitudes toward institutions can shift. Between 2015 and 2017, "the share of Republicans who said colleges and universities were having a negative effect on the way things were going in the U.S. rose from 37% to 58%," illustrating how partisan identity can reshape perceptions of previously respected institutions almost overnight.

Institutional Strengths and Weaknesses Exposed

The MAGA era has served as an unprecedented stress test for American democratic institutions, revealing both remarkable resilience and alarming vulnerabilities. The results paint a complex picture of a system that proved more fragile in some areas and more robust in others than many observers expected.

On the fragility side, scholars noted that "the systematic underutilization of power by presidents and congressional majorities has long served as a vital source of democratic stability in the United States," but this restraint proved to be more dependent on informal norms than formal rules. When those norms were challenged or abandoned, the constitutional system's formal checks and balances often proved inadequate to prevent institutional damage.

The federal bureaucracy—often derided as the "deep state" by movement supporters—demonstrated surprising resilience in some areas while proving vulnerable in others. Career civil servants in agencies like the Department of Agriculture successfully protected climate research from political interference, showing that professional cultures and internal networks can provide meaningful protection for institutional integrity. However, the "push to reduce civil service headcount combined with a much deeper than usual politicization of the remaining bureaucracy" threatens "a widespread deterioration in the quality and effectiveness of the US civil service."

Perhaps most significantly, Trump succeeded in making "widespread appointments" to the federal judiciary, including "three justices to the US Supreme Court, 54 United States Circuit Court of Appeals judges, and 174 federal District Court judges." These lifetime appointments represent the movement's most enduring institutional legacy, with effects that will persist long after current political alignments have shifted.

The electoral system itself proved both vulnerable and resilient. While Trump's refusal to "publicly concede defeat" and his campaign's "dozens of unsuccessful lawsuits to challenge the results" represented unprecedented challenges to democratic norms, the system ultimately held. State and local election officials, many of them Republicans, maintained professional integrity under enormous pressure. Federal and state courts, including Trump-appointed judges, rejected unfounded legal challenges.

However, the stress testing also revealed dangerous weaknesses. Polling shows that "more than a third of people polled supported reducing presidential powers—37 percent in February 2025," representing "a 12 point jump from when we asked the question in December 2023," suggesting growing concern about executive overreach among the general public.

The media landscape emerged as particularly vulnerable to institutional degradation. Public confidence in "the national news media" fell to just "13 percent," reflecting both deliberate attacks on press credibility and broader changes in how Americans consume information. This represents a critical vulnerability, as democratic accountability depends heavily on independent journalism.

Competing Visions of National Success

The MAGA era has crystallized fundamentally different visions of what American success should look like, revealing tensions that go to the heart of national identity. These competing visions extend far beyond traditional left-right political disagreements, encompassing different understandings of America's role in history, its relationship to the rest of the world, and the proper balance between individual liberty and collective responsibility.

The MAGA worldview "builds on a narrative of national decline, arguing that America has lost its former greatness due to globalization, immigration, multiculturalism, and foreign influence." This diagnosis leads to prescriptions focused on economic nationalism, cultural traditionalism, and America First foreign policy. Success, in this framework, means restoring the country to an idealized version of its past, protecting American workers from global competition, and prioritizing national sovereignty over international cooperation.

The alternative vision, embraced by many Americans across party lines, sees greatness as lying ahead rather than behind. This perspective views globalization as creating opportunities for American leadership, sees diversity as a source of strength rather than division, and believes that America's influence is best exercised through multilateral institutions and soft power. Success means adapting to changing global realities while maintaining American values and leadership.

These competing visions extend to domestic policy as well. The MAGA approach calls for "dramatic expansion and consolidation of presidential power over the executive branch" justified by "the unitary executive theory," while the alternative vision emphasizes checks and balances, independent institutions, and distributed power.

Economic policy reveals similar divides. The MAGA approach prioritizes "reciprocal tariffs" and reducing the federal government by "firing 'corrupt bureaucrats,'" while the alternative emphasizes international trade, regulated markets, and professional civil service. Economists note that "there will be offsetting pluses and minuses" from these different approaches, with "the net economic impacts most likely somewhere in between the most pessimistic prognostications and the rosy scenario."

Perhaps most fundamentally, these competing visions reflect different theories of democracy itself. The MAGA vision emphasizes direct popular will, executive leadership, and majoritarian decision-making. The alternative vision emphasizes constitutional protections, minority rights, and institutional mediation of popular will. Both can claim democratic legitimacy, but they point toward very different futures for American governance.

The challenge for American democracy is that "majority of Republicans nationally identify as MAGA for first time," while substantial portions of the population remain committed to alternative visions. This creates a fundamental tension about the direction of the country that cannot be easily resolved through normal political processes.

America's Role in a Changing Global Landscape

The MAGA movement's impact on America's global position may prove to be its most consequential legacy. International observers note that "the US's more nationalist outlook and disruptive foreign policy since Donald Trump took office for the second time in early 2025" represents a fundamental shift away from the post-World War II consensus about American global leadership.

This shift comes at a critical moment in global affairs. Analysts describe the current situation as one where "there is no single world order — only disorder and competing visions of dominance." The traditional Western-led international system faces challenges from rising powers, particularly China, which seeks to "exercise leadership" through BRICS and other alternative institutions while opposing "Western states imposing their values on other states."

America's "retreat from global leadership – and, in particular, its rejection of soft power – has created an opening for China to position itself as a stabilizing force in an increasingly turbulent world." This represents a dramatic reversal from the American approach that defined the post-Cold War era. The rapid cuts to foreign assistance and withdrawal from multilateral institutions amount to "a swift undoing of decades of U.S. foreign policy posture in only three months."

European allies have been particularly affected by this shift. "The Biden administration had lulled Europeans into a belief that the first Trump administration was an exception to the rule of sound US leadership," but Trump's return has forced a fundamental recalculation of transatlantic relationships. European leaders now face the prospect of providing their own security guarantees and global leadership without reliable American partnership.

The economic dimensions of this shift are equally significant. The emphasis on tariffs and economic nationalism risks "a loss of confidence in US governance" among international partners and investors. The administration's approach "has caused long-lasting damage to one of the foundational pillars of U.S. economic strength: stability."

However, American retreat also creates opportunities. While "there is little sign that the quest for such autonomy has been accompanied by a realistic alternative to the US or China as a provider of global public goods," other nations and institutions may step into leadership roles on issues like climate change, global health, and economic development.

The ultimate question is whether this represents a temporary shift or a permanent reorientation of America's global role. Some observers see this as part of "a 75-year cycle in decline, where the institutions that once defined Western dominance" are "increasingly out of sync with the realities of power." If so, America may need to find new ways to exercise influence in a more multipolar world.

Looking Forward: Scenarios for American Greatness

As Americans look toward the future, several possible paths emerge from the tensions and revelations of the MAGA era. Each represents a different resolution of the fundamental questions the movement has raised about American identity, institutions, and global role.

The first scenario involves the successful institutionalization of MAGA principles within the Republican Party and their gradual acceptance by broader American society. With "Trump's victory in the 2024 election, the principles and priorities of the MAGA movement, especially its devotion to Trump, became even more important to Republican candidates and office holders." This path would likely lead to a more nationalist, inward-looking America with stronger executive power, reduced international commitments, and a more culturally traditionalist domestic policy framework.

A second scenario involves the movement's gradual moderation and integration into conventional political institutions. Some observers note that "Trump has never really expanded support much beyond himself" and question whether "those who crossed over to vote for him in 2024, who don't consider themselves MAGA" will "stick with the party." In this scenario, the more extreme elements of MAGA would fade while some policy preferences become normalized.

A third possibility is continued polarization and institutional conflict, with neither vision achieving clear dominance. This could lead to a semi-permanent state of political instability, with institutions weakened by constant partisan warfare and the country struggling to address long-term challenges requiring sustained national effort.

The fourth scenario involves some form of democratic breakdown or transformation, either through the concentration of power in executive institutions or through the fragmentation of the country into more autonomous regions with different governing philosophies. Some scholars warn that "we are no longer living in a democratic regime" and express concern about authoritarian consolidation.

The path ultimately taken will depend on several factors: the movement's ability to maintain unity and purpose after Trump's eventual departure from politics; the capacity of democratic institutions to adapt and respond to legitimate grievances; the willingness of political leaders to prioritize democratic norms over partisan advantage; and the ability of Americans to find common ground despite deep differences.

CONCLUSION

The MAGA movement has forced Americans to confront fundamental questions that previous generations took for granted. What does it mean to be American in a globalized world? How much economic disruption can democratic societies absorb before they begin to fracture? Can diverse societies maintain enough social cohesion to govern themselves effectively? What obligations do successful nations have to the broader international community?

These questions have no easy answers, and the MAGA era has demonstrated that Americans hold genuinely different views about each of them. The movement's greatest contribution may be forcing the country to grapple explicitly with these tensions rather than pretending they don't exist.

The future of American greatness will likely depend not on resolving these tensions completely—which may be impossible in a diverse democracy—but on finding ways to manage them constructively. This requires institutions strong enough to channel conflict productively, leaders committed to democratic norms even when they prove inconvenient, and citizens willing to engage with those who hold fundamentally different views about the country's future.

The MAGA movement has shown that American democracy is both more fragile and more resilient than many believed. It can survive unprecedented challenges to its norms and institutions, but it cannot take its survival for granted. The lessons of this era must inform how Americans approach the equally challenging questions that lie ahead, from technological disruption to climate change to demographic transformation.

In the end, the true test of American greatness may not be whether the country returns to some imagined golden age or achieves some predetermined vision of progress, but whether it can adapt to changing circumstances while maintaining its democratic character and capacity for self-renewal. The MAGA era has been part of that ongoing test, and the results are still being written.